Better Homes and Gardens®

Kids' Snacks

© Copyright 1985 by Meredith Corporation, Des Moines, Iowa.
All Rights Reserved. Printed in the United States of America.
First Edition. Second Printing, 1985.
Library of Congress Catalog Card Number: 84-61309
ISBN: 0-696-01482-3 (hard cover)
ISBN: 0-696-01480-7 (trade paperback)

BETTER HOMES AND GARDENS® BOOKS

Editor: Gerald M. Knox
Art Director: Ernest Shelton
Managing Editor: David A. Kirchner

Food and Nutrition Editor: Nancy Byal
Department Head, Cook Books: Sharyl Heiken
Associate Department Heads: Sandra Granseth,
     Rosemary C. Hutchinson, Elizabeth Woolever
Senior Food Editors: Julia Malloy, Marcia Stanley,
     Joyce Trollope
Associate Food Editors: Barbara Atkins, Molly Culbertson,
     Linda Foley, Linda Henry, Lynn Hoppe, Jill Johnson,
     Mary Jo Plutt, Maureen Powers
Recipe Development Editor: Marion Viall
Test Kitchen Director: Sharon Stilwell
Test Kitchen Photo Studio Director: Janet Pittman
Test Kitchen Home Economists: Jean Brekke, Kay Cargill,
     Marilyn Cornelius, Maryellyn Krantz, Lynelle Munn,
     Dianna Nolin, Marge Steenson, Cynthia Volcko

Associate Art Directors: Linda Ford Vermie,
     Neoma Alt West, Randall Yontz
Copy and Production Editors: Marsha Jahns,
     Mary Helen Schiltz, Carl Voss, David A. Walsh
Assistant Art Directors: Faith Berven, Harijs Priekulis,
     Tom Wegner
Senior Graphic Designers: Alisann Dixon,
     Lynda Haupert, Lyne Neymeyer
Graphic Designers: Mike Burns, Mike Eagleton, Deb Miner,
     Stan Sams, Darla Whipple-Frain

Vice President, Editorial Director: Doris Eby
Executive Director, Editorial Services: Duane L. Gregg

General Manager: Fred Stines
Director of Publishing: Robert B. Nelson
Vice President, Retail Marketing: Jamie Martin
Vice President, Direct Marketing: Arthur Heydendael

KIDS' SNACKS

Editor: Jill Johnson
Copy and Production Editor: Mary Helen Schiltz
Graphic Designer: Stan Sams
Contributing Photographer: Mike Dieter
Food Stylists: Jill Mead, Janet Pittman
Electronic Text Processor: Donna Russell

Our seal assures you that every recipe in *Kids' Snacks* has
been tested in the Better Homes and Gardens® Test Kitchen.
This means that each recipe is practical and reliable, and meets
our high standards of taste appeal.

On the cover: *Creamy Coolers* (see recipe, page 28)

Contents

Treat Your Kids Right

Kids and snacks...they're a perfect combination. At a time when kids are growing fast and playing hard, nutritious snacks between meals can give them the nourishment boost they need. We designed the recipes in *Kids' Snacks* to give them that boost, in a way that's easy and fun for both you and the kids.

First we figured that for a snack to make it past a kid's nose, it has to look and taste good. So we created over a hundred wholesome and delicious recipes and tried out each one on several children before we put it in this book. Most of the kids couldn't tell the snacks were good for them. They just knew they liked what they were eating. (Look for the youngsters' own comments alongside many of the recipes.)

We also knew that when kids want a snack, they want it right away. So we made the recipes easy and quick for adults to fix (or fix ahead). Some recipes are so simple, kids can make them by themselves. You'll recognize these by the "Kids' Recipe" stamp, like those in the bottom right-hand corner of the next page.

Finally, we thought that snacks should be something kids look forward to. So we packed ours full of fun. Flip through the pages of the book and you'll see what we mean. Of course, looking is only the beginning. Making and eating the snacks is the best part of all!

Pizza Pitas
(see recipe, page 19)

(marbles)

Flying Saucers
(see recipe, page 57)

Flip-Flop Bars
(see recipe, page 69)

Tangled Bread
(see recipe, page 74)

Potato Salad Chips
(see recipe, page 13)

Three Blind Mice Crackers
(see recipe, page 15)

Fancy Hats
(see recipe, page 77)

(Kids' Recipe stamp)

Nibblin' Fish

2½ cups round toasted oat
　　cereal
1½ cups pretzel sticks
　1 cup small fish-shape
　　crackers
　1 cup mixed nuts *or* peanuts

● In a 13x9x2-inch baking pan combine oat cereal, pretzel sticks, fish-shape crackers, and nuts.

Fishin' for a nibble? You'll need pretzel sticks for fishing poles to catch the fish-shape crackers, nuts for stones that the fish can hide behind, and round cereal for air bubbles to let you know where the fish are lurking.

⅓ cup cooking oil
2 teaspoons Worcestershire
　　sauce

● Stir together oil and Worcestershire sauce; drizzle over cereal mixture, tossing to coat evenly.
　Bake in a 300° oven for 30 minutes, stirring occasionally. Cool. Store mixture in a tightly covered container. Makes about 6 cups.

Maple Syrup Granola

1½ cups regular rolled oats ½ cup Grape Nuts cereal ½ cup peanuts ¼ cup sesame seed ¼ cup coconut	● In a bowl stir together rolled oats, Grape Nuts cereal, peanuts, sesame seed, and coconut.
⅔ cup maple-flavored syrup ¼ cup butter *or* margarine, melted	● Stir in syrup and melted butter or margarine. Spread mixture in a greased 15x10x1-inch baking pan. Bake in a 375° oven for 20 minutes, stirring once.
½ cup raisins	● Transfer to a bowl. Stir in raisins. Cool. Store in a tightly covered container. Makes about 4 cups.

At our kids' taste panel, Kristin liked this granola because it reminded her of the topping on apple crisp. Charley thought it would be good as a breakfast cereal, a dessert after lunch, or an after-school snack.

Graham Cracker Sandwiches

EQUIPMENT
table knife

3 graham crackers Peanut butter Ground cinnamon	● Break each graham cracker into two squares. Use a table knife to spread each square lightly with some peanut butter. Sprinkle each with a little cinnamon.
1 small banana	● Peel the banana; throw away the peel. Use the table knife to cut the banana into ¼-inch slices. Arrange the banana slices on *half* of the graham cracker squares. Top with the rest of the graham cracker squares, peanut butter side down. Press together gently. Makes 3.

Is your stomach growling so loud you can't hear yourself think? Stop the noise in a jiffy with these *Graham Cracker Sandwiches* that have peanut butter and banana on the inside. The recipe makes three, so you can cure three growling stomachs at once.

Mama-Mia Popcorn

8 cups popped popcorn (6 tablespoons unpopped) 2 tablespoons butter *or* margarine, melted	● Place popcorn in a large mixing bowl. Drizzle melted butter or margarine over popcorn; toss to coat.
1 teaspoon Italian salad dressing mix	● Add the dry salad dressing mix. Toss gently till well mixed. Makes 8 cups.

"It's better than plain popcorn," the kids told us. And it's not much harder to make. Let kids use their hands to toss buttered popcorn with Italian salad dressing mix.

Bite-Size Pizzas

6 melba toast rounds 1 tablespoon cooked bacon pieces 3 cherry tomatoes, halved	● Place melba toast rounds on a baking sheet. Place *½ teaspoon* cooked bacon pieces atop *each* melba toast round. Place a cherry tomato half, cut side down, on each round.	**Watch out for squirting tomatoes with each bite!** **MICROWAVE TIMING** Place cheese-topped melba toast rounds in a circle on a nonmetal plate. Micro-cook on HIGH (100%) power about 30 seconds or till the cheese is melted. Cool 5 minutes before serving.
1 slice process Swiss cheese *or* American cheese	● Cut cheese slice into six equal pieces. Place one piece over each tomato. Broil 4 inches from heat for 1 to 2 minutes or just till cheese is melted. Cool 5 minutes before serving. Makes 6.	

Peanut Poppers

4 cups popped popcorn (3 tablespoons unpopped) ½ cup peanuts ¼ cup raisins	● In a medium mixing bowl stir together popcorn, peanuts, and raisins.	**Popcorn! Peanuts! Raisins! Each is a great snack by itself. Toss them all together with melted peanut butter for a finger-lickin' snack that's three times as good as one of them alone.**
1 tablespoon butter *or* margarine 1 tablespoon peanut butter	● In a small saucepan combine butter or margarine and peanut butter. Heat and stir over medium heat till melted. Pour peanut butter mixture over popcorn mixture. Toss to coat. Makes about 4½ cups.	

Chinatown Snack

1 3-ounce can chow mein noodles 2 cups bite-size rice squares cereal ¾ cup peanuts	● In a 13x9x2-inch baking pan combine chow mein noodles, cereal, and peanuts.	**Skip the chopsticks and use your fingers to eat this snack of squiggly chow mein noodles, square rice cereal, and peanuts.**
¼ cup cooking oil 2 teaspoons soy sauce ⅛ teaspoon garlic powder	● Stir together oil, soy sauce, and garlic powder; drizzle over chow mein noodle mixture. Toss till well coated. Bake in a 300° oven for 20 minutes, stirring occasionally. Cool. Store in a tightly covered container. Makes about 4½ cups.	

German Chocolate Crunch

8 cups bite-size wheat *or* rice squares cereal ⅔ cup coarsely chopped pecans ½ cup flaked coconut	● In a 13x9x2-inch baking pan stir together cereal, chopped pecans, and coconut. Set aside.
1 6-ounce package semisweet chocolate pieces 2 tablespoons butter *or* margarine ¼ cup light corn syrup 2 tablespoons brown sugar	● In a saucepan melt semisweet chocolate pieces and butter or margarine over low heat, stirring frequently. Stir in corn syrup and brown sugar. Cook and stir over low heat till sugar is dissolved. Pour chocolate mixture over cereal mixture, tossing to coat evenly. Bake in a 300° oven for 15 to 20 minutes, stirring twice. Pour into a large bowl to cool. Store in a tightly covered container. Makes about 9 cups.

Though her front teeth were missing, Janelle didn't let that keep her from tasting this crunchy cereal snack. Try it as an easier, less-filling alternative to German chocolate cake.

Naturally Good Nachos

2 5½-inch flour tortillas	● With kitchen scissors cut each tortilla into four wedges, as shown below. Place on an ungreased baking sheet. Bake in a 350° oven 10 to 12 minutes or till crisp.
2 slices American cheese 4 teaspoons chopped green pepper	● Cut each cheese slice into four triangles. Place one cheese triangle on each tortilla wedge. Top each with ½ teaspoon chopped green pepper. Bake in the 350° oven 4 to 6 minutes more or till cheese is melted. Makes 8.

Instead of using tortilla chips from the store to make nachos, make your own unsalted, greaseless chips from flour tortillas. Sound hard to do? It's not! See how easy it is in the photo below.

Cut each tortilla into four wedges with kitchen scissors. Put them on a baking sheet and bake till they're crisp.

Cinnamon Snails

4 slices soft-texture whole wheat *or* white bread

¼ cup soft-style cream cheese

● Trim the crusts from the bread slices (step 1). Spread *1 tablespoon* of the cream cheese on *each* slice of bread (step 2).

Roll up bread slices with cream cheese on the inside (step 3). Cut each roll into thirds (step 4).

These snails have a crispy cinnamon "shell" on the outside. Inside you'll find a creamy pinwheel of cream cheese. For even more flavor, use soft-style cream cheese that's flavored with pineapple or strawberry.

3 tablespoons sugar

1½ teaspoons ground cinnamon

¼ cup butter *or* margarine, melted

● Stir together sugar and cinnamon till well mixed. Dip each cut roll into the melted butter or margarine (step 5), then into the sugar-cinnamon mixture (step 6). Do not dip the ends of the rolls. Place rolls, seam side down, on an ungreased baking sheet (step 7).

Bake in a 350° oven about 12 minutes or till light brown and crisp. Serve warm or cool. Makes 12.

5

7   **6**

S'more Gorp

2 cups honey graham cereal
1 cup tiny marshmallows
1 cup peanuts
½ cup semisweet chocolate
    pieces
½ cup raisins

EQUIPMENT
medium paper sack   measuring cups
    or plastic bag

● In a medium paper sack or a large plastic bag combine the cereal, marshmallows, peanuts, chocolate pieces, and raisins. Close the end of the bag and shake well. Store the mixture in a closed plastic bag or a tightly covered container. Makes about 5 cups.

S'mores are gooey treats made by sandwiching roasted marshmallows and chocolate between graham crackers. This handy treat gives you the same s'more flavors without the mess. Just shake everything together in a bag.

Curly Taco Mix

Pictured on page 35.

¼ cup butter *or* margarine
1 teaspoon chili powder
½ teaspoon ground cumin

● In a 13x9x2-inch baking pan heat butter or margarine in a 300° oven for 3 to 5 minutes or till melted. Remove pan; stir in chili powder and cumin.

3 cups small corn chips
2 cups puffed cheese curls
1 cup shelled pumpkin seed *or* peanuts

● Add corn chips, puffed cheese curls, and shelled pumpkin seed or peanuts. Stir to mix thoroughly.
   Bake in the 300° oven for 15 minutes, stirring once or twice. Cool. Store in a tightly covered container. Makes 5 cups.

MICROWAVE TIMING
In a large nonmetal bowl micro-cook butter on HIGH (100%) power about 1 minute or till melted. Stir in chili powder and ground cumin. Add remaining ingredients; stir well. Micro-cook on HIGH (100%) power for 6 minutes, stirring every 2 minutes. Cool.

Potato Salad Chips

Pictured on page 5.

1 hard-cooked egg

● With an egg slicer or sharp knife, thinly slice the hard-cooked egg.

8 to 10 potato chips
   Mayonnaise *or* salad dressing
8 to 10 dill *or* sweet pickle slices
   Paprika

● Spread potato chips with a little mayonnaise or salad dressing. Top each with a pickle slice and an egg slice. Sprinkle with paprika. Serve immediately. Makes 8 to 10.

Top plain potato chips to make them taste like potato salad! Let kids pile on the pickles, egg slices, and paprika.
   Use thick or rippled potato chips for the crispiest snack.

Shake-a-Sack Cracker Snack

EQUIPMENT

medium paper sack or plastic bag	measuring cups measuring spoons

3 cups small square cheese crackers
3 cups oyster crackers
2 cups bite-size pretzel nuggets
1 0.4-ounce package buttermilk salad dressing mix
½ teaspoon dried dillweed *or* dried oregano, crushed

● In a medium paper sack or a large plastic bag combine the cheese crackers, oyster crackers, pretzel nuggets, the dry buttermilk salad dressing mix, and the dillweed or oregano. Close the end of the bag and shake till everything is mixed together well.

The hardest thing about this snack is saying the name. If you can't say it right, don't worry. Just put everything in a sack, shake it up, and munch.

¼ cup cooking oil

● Pour the oil into the paper sack or plastic bag and shake well again. Store in a closed plastic bag or a tightly covered container. Makes about 8 cups.

Crowded Canoes

kids' recipe

EQUIPMENT

cutting board	paper towel
table knife	waxed paper

1 celery stalk	● On a cutting board use a table knife to cut the leafy end and the stem end from the celery. Throw away the ends. Rinse the celery stalk under cold running water. Pat dry with a paper towel. Cut the stalk into three equal pieces.
Any flavor cheese spread	● With the knife spread the cheese spread into the groove of the celery stalk, piling it up a little bit.
1 to 2 tablespoons crisp rice cereal *or* corn puff cereal	● Spread the cereal on a sheet of waxed paper. Gently press the celery pieces, cheese side down, into the cereal. Lift up. If the cereal didn't stick well, press again. Makes 3.

Except for the crunchy cereal on top, this was a familiar snack to the kids who tasted it. They told us to tell you that peanut butter in the middle of the celery is tasty, too.

Pirate's Treasure

¾ cup all-purpose flour 1 5-ounce jar American cheese spread ¼ cup butter *or* margarine, softened	● In a medium mixing bowl combine flour, cheese spread, and softened butter or margarine. Mix with your hands till well combined.
1 cup corn flakes, finely crushed (½ cup)	● Spread crushed corn flakes on a piece of waxed paper. Shape cheese mixture into 1-inch balls by rolling small amounts between palms of hands. Roll in crushed corn flakes to coat. Place about 2 inches apart on an ungreased cookie sheet. 　With the bottom of a drinking glass, flatten balls to ¼-inch thickness. Bake in a 375° oven about 12 minutes or till edges are lightly browned. Makes 24.

These crisp cheese wafers are called *Pirate's Treasure* because, as eight-year-old Verity explained, "They look like gold coins."

Little hands can help mix the dough because it's soft but not sticky.

Three Blind Mice Crackers

Pictured on page 5.

4 slices melba toast 6 whole pitted olives, halved lengthwise; 3 cherry tomatoes, quartered; *or* 12 whole almonds	● Place melba toast slices on a baking sheet. For mice, arrange *three* olive halves, tomato quarters, or whole almonds on *each* slice of melba toast.
2 slices American cheese Chow mein noodles	● Cut cheese slices in half to fit melba toast. Place a cheese strip atop "mice" on melba toast. Broil about 4 inches from heat for 1 to 3 minutes or till cheese melts. Insert a chow mein noodle under cheese near each "mouse" for tails. Makes 4.

Three little mice made of olives, tomatoes, or almonds are hiding all but their tails under a cover of melted cheese.

MICROWAVE TIMING

Place cheese-topped crackers on a nonmetal plate. Micro-cook on HIGH (100%) power for 30 seconds or till cheese is melted. Remove and insert chow mein noodles for tails.

Cheese Ball Beach Balls

kids' recipe

EQUIPMENT

small mixing bowl	ruler
fork	cereal bowl

1 3-ounce package cream cheese	● Take the cream cheese out of the refrigerator. Let it stand on the counter for 30 minutes so it will be easy to mix.
½ of a 4-ounce package (½ cup) shredded cheddar *or* mozzarella cheese	● In a small mixing bowl place the softened cream cheese and the shredded cheese that you want to use. Mash the cheeses together with a fork till they are well mixed.
¼ cup sunflower nuts	● Stir in the sunflower nuts. Shape the cheese mixture into 1-inch balls by rolling small amounts between the palms of your hands.
¼ to ⅓ cup Grape Nuts cereal	● Put the Grape Nuts cereal in a cereal bowl. Roll each cheese ball in the cereal till it's coated. Eat right away or store in a tightly covered container in the refrigerator till you're ready to eat them. Makes 12.

When Sonya looked at the plate of little cheese balls she'd made, she said they looked like sand-covered beach balls. That's how these good-for-you snacks got their name.

   Sonya thought the hardest part about making this recipe was mixing together the two cheeses. If you think you'd like help with that part of the recipe, grab a grown-up.

Kabob-o'-Links

10 toothpicks
10 ½-inch cubes cheddar, Swiss, mozzarella, *or* Monterey Jack cheese (1 ounce)
1 *or* 2 frankfurters, cut into ½-inch slices; ten ½-inch cubes fully cooked ham; *or* 5 cocktail weiners, halved crosswise
1 *or* 2 whole dill *or* sweet pickles, cut into ½-inch slices; 10 green *or* ripe olives; *or* 1 small stalk celery, cut into ½-inch slices

● On each toothpick thread one cheese cube; one frankfurter slice, ham cube, or cocktail weiner half; and one pickle slice, olive, or celery slice. To store, cover and refrigerate. Makes 10.

The kids who tasted these treats on a toothpick said, "They look like shish kabobs!" Choose the cheese, meat, and relish you're sure your kid will like and let him spear one of each on a toothpick.

Silly-Shape Cheese

Mix playtime with snack-time to encourage kids to munch wholesome foods, such as cheese, that they might not otherwise eat.

All you need is cookie cutters and your kids' favorite kind of sliced cheese. Let them press the cookie cutters into the cheese to make all sorts of shapes. They can eat the shapes plain or arrange them on crackers or bread. They'll find that the "scraps" the cookie cutters left behind are fun to nibble, too.

Cheese Carrots

1 3-ounce package cream cheese	● Place the cream cheese in a small mixer bowl; let stand at room temperature for 30 minutes to soften.
1 cup finely shredded cheddar cheese (4 ounces) **2 teaspoons honey** **1 large carrot, finely shredded (½ cup)**	● In the bowl beat cream cheese, cheddar cheese, and honey till blended. Stir in ½ cup finely shredded carrot. Cover and chill for 1 hour. Shape the cheese mixture into 2½-inch logs; taper one end of each log to look like a carrot.
1 large carrot, finely shredded (½ cup) **Parsley sprigs**	● Spread ½ cup finely shredded carrot on a piece of waxed paper. Roll each cheese "carrot" in the shredded carrot, pressing lightly to coat. Just before serving, insert parsley sprigs into the wide end of each carrot. To store, cover and refrigerate. Makes 10.

Carrots are a rabbit's favorite snack, but these make-believe carrots are especially for kids. Let your little ones nibble them with crispy crackers.

Peanut Butter Faceups

- Toast the bread, if desired.
- In a bowl mix 2 tablespoons *peanut butter* with a Mix-In. Spread the mixture on the bread.
- Top with a Sprinkle-On. Makes 1.

If you tried all of the different combinations listed below, you could eat a different peanut butter sandwich Monday through Saturday for the next 2 years!

## Breads	+ ## Mix-Ins	+ ## Sprinkle-Ons
1 slice white bread	1 tablespoon honey	1 tablespoon raisins
1 slice whole wheat bread	1 tablespoon jelly *or* jam	1 tablespoon sunflower nuts
1 slice raisin bread	1 tablespoon maple-flavored syrup	1 tablespoon peanut halves *or* chopped peanuts
1 slice French bread	1 tablespoon orange juice	1 tablespoon crisp rice cereal
1 small pita bread round, split	1 tablespoon applesauce	1 heaping tablespoon granola
½ split hamburger bun	1 tablespoon mashed banana	1 tablespoon coconut
½ split hot dog bun	1 tablespoon drained crushed pineapple	1 tablespoon alfalfa sprouts
½ split English muffin		1 tablespoon shredded carrot
½ split bagel		1 teaspoon sesame seed
		Several dashes ground cinnamon

Inside-Out Sandwiches

EQUIPMENT

small bowl	small spoon
measuring spoons	table knife

Have you ever seen a sandwich with bread on the inside and meat on the outside? It may sound crazy, but it's fun to eat and it sure tastes good.

2 tablespoons cheese spread (any flavor) 2 teaspoons mayonnaise *or* salad dressing ¼ teaspoon prepared mustard	● If the cheese spread is in the refrigerator, take it out and let it stand on the counter about 15 minutes so it will be easy to mix. In a small bowl use a spoon to stir together the cheese spread, mayonnaise or salad dressing, and mustard. Set it aside.
2 slices firm-texture bread	● With a table knife, carefully cut the crusts from the bread slices. (Use the crusts to feed birds.) Spread the cheese mixture on one side of a bread slice. Top with the other bread slice. Cut the sandwich into five long strips.
1 2½-ounce package very thinly sliced pressed smoked chicken, ham, turkey, corned beef, *or* pastrami	● For each sandwich, use *two* meat slices. Lay one meat slice on top of another slice so that half of the bottom one is covered. (Look at the drawing at right if you need help.) Put one sandwich strip on the edge of the meat, as the drawing shows you. Roll up the sandwich strip inside the meat. Do the same thing with the other bread strips and meat slices to make five. Wrap any leftover meat slices in plastic wrap and put in the refrigerator to use another time. Makes 5.

Pizza Pitas

Pictured on page 5.

Crisp on the edges and chewy in the middle, these little pizzas taste a lot like the big kind.

1 small pita bread round	● Split pita bread round in half, forming two thin circles.
2 tablespoons catsup, pizza sauce, *or* spaghetti sauce ⅛ teaspoon dried oregano, crushed 2 tablespoons finely chopped salami, pepperoni, summer sausage, *or* bologna ¼ cup shredded mozzarella *or* cheddar cheese	● Spread *each* circle with *half* of the catsup or sauce. Sprinkle *half* of the oregano over *each*. Top *each* circle with *half* of the meat and *half* of the cheese. Place pita bread halves on a baking sheet. Bake in a 375° oven for 8 to 10 minutes or till cheese is bubbly and edges of pita bread are crisp. Remove from baking sheet; cool slightly. Makes 2.

Sunflower Sandwich

Pictured on page 4.

Sunflower seeds come from the center of sunflowers and are a good snack by themselves. If you like, use them for a final touch on this snack-time work of art.

EQUIPMENT
table knife

**½ of a split English muffin
or hamburger bun, *or*
1 slice bread
Peanut butter**

● Use a table knife to spread English muffin half, hamburger bun half, or bread slice with peanut butter.

**1 canned pineapple slice,
cut into 8 pieces, *or*
canned pineapple
tidbits
Raisins
Sunflower nuts
(if you like)**

● Arrange the pineapple pieces on top of the peanut butter in a circle to look like the petals of a flower.
   Fill the center of the flower with raisins. If you like, sprinkle with sunflower nuts. Makes 1.

Banana in a Bun

This snack is like a banana split in a hot dog bun. A whole sandwich might be too filling, so split each one in half and share with your friends.

EQUIPMENT
table knife   small spoon

**2 hot dog buns
Peanut butter**

● Open hot dog buns. With a table knife spread peanut butter on inside of buns.

1 small banana

● Peel the banana; throw away the peel. With the table knife thinly slice banana crosswise into circles; arrange on *one side* of each open bun.

**Your favorite jam *or* jelly
Raisins, chopped peanuts,
or miniature semisweet
chocolate pieces**

● Spoon jam or jelly over peanut butter on the other side of each bun. Sprinkle jelly side with raisins, peanuts, or chocolate pieces.
   Close bun. Cut each bun in half crosswise. Makes 4 servings.

Breakfast in Bread

1 **egg** 2 **tablespoons milk**	● In a shallow bowl, with a fork beat together egg and milk. Set aside.
½ **cup corn flakes**	● In a small plastic bag crush corn flakes to measure ¼ cup. Spread on a sheet of waxed paper. Set aside.
2 **slices bread** **Butter *or* margarine** 1 **slice boiled ham**	● Spread one side of each bread slice with butter or margarine. Place boiled ham on the buttered side of one slice of bread. Top with the other slice of bread, buttered side down. Cut the sandwich diagonally into quarters.
1 **tablespoon butter *or* margarine**	● Dip the sandwich quarters into the egg mixture, then into the crushed corn flakes to coat. In a skillet melt 1 tablespoon butter or margarine over medium heat. Cook sandwich quarters about 2 minutes on each side or till light brown. Transfer to serving plates.
Maple-flavored syrup	● Serve with maple-flavored syrup. Makes 2 servings.

We called this snack *Breakfast in Bread* because we made it from such breakfast favorites as corn flakes, ham, an egg, bread, and maple syrup. According to our tasters, it tastes like French toast, and would be good as a late-morning snack or in the afternoon after a hard day of play.

Pita Rabbit

¼ **cup peanut butter** 2 **teaspoons mayonnaise *or* salad dressing** ¼ **cup shredded carrot** 2 **tablespoons raisins**	● In a small bowl stir together peanut butter and mayonnaise or salad dressing. Stir in shredded carrot and raisins.
2 **small pita bread rounds** ¼ **cup fresh alfalfa sprouts**	● Cut pita rounds in half crosswise. Fill *each* half with *one-fourth* of the peanut butter mixture, spreading evenly. Stuff *each* pita half with *one-fourth* of the alfalfa sprouts. Makes 2 servings.

Carrots and sprouts may be a rabbit's weaknesses, but peanut butter is the weakness of many a kid. Stirred together and stuffed into tiny pita pockets, peanut butter, carrots, and sprouts make a tasty treat—and a healthy one besides.

Tuna Schooners

1 3¼-ounce can tuna, drained and flaked ¼ cup mayonnaise *or* salad dressing ¼ cup chopped apple 2 tablespoons sunflower nuts	● In a small mixing bowl combine tuna, mayonnaise or salad dressing, chopped apple, and sunflower nuts. Mix well. If desired, cover and chill.
2 whole grain English muffins	● Split and toast the English muffins. On *each* muffin half, spread *one-fourth* of the tuna mixture.
8 triangular tortilla chips	● For sails, insert *two* tortilla chips, short side down, into the tuna mixture on *each* muffin. Makes 4 servings.

Kids will go overboard about this smooth-sailing snack, with sails made of tortilla chips and a cargo of tuna, chopped apple, and sunflower nuts.

Tuna Schooners

Awfully Good Waffle
(see recipe, page 25)

Sleeping Pickle
(see recipe, page 25)

Hill o' Beans Sandwich

1 slice bread
⅓ cup barbecue beans *or* pork and beans in tomato sauce, drained

● Place bread slice on an ungreased baking sheet. Spread beans on bread slice so that the top of the bread is completely covered and the beans are slightly mounded in center.

½ of a 1½-ounce slice mozzarella cheese

● Cut cheese slice diagonally into quarters; arrange atop beans.
   Bake in a 425° oven for 6 to 7 minutes or till the cheese melts. Serve warm. Makes 1.

Is that smidgen of pork and beans leftover from last night's supper so small it isn't worth a hill o' beans? Put it to good use in this hot and hasty snackwich.

Eating One Kind of Bread Can Get Stale

Keep your kids from getting stuck in the rut of eating the same kind of bread day in and day out. Introduce them to a variety of bread tastes and textures, starting at snack time with these *Slaphappy Snackwiches*.
   More than ever before, grocery stores are stocking an incredible variety of breads. You'll find whole wheat, cracked wheat, wheat berry, pumpernickel, oatmeal, granola, and more. There are also English muffins, bagels, pita bread rounds, and whole grain hamburger and hot dog buns. Sneak one of these special breads into your kid's next snackwich. He'll think it's the greatest thing since sliced bread!

Awfully Good Waffle

Pictured on pages 22 and 23.

EQUIPMENT
toaster	table knife

1 frozen waffle	● Toast the waffle in the toaster.
Soft-style cream cheese **Any flavor preserves, jam,** **or jelly**	● Lightly spread cream cheese on the waffle so all the holes are filled. Lightly spread preserves, jam, or jelly over the cream cheese. Makes 1 serving.

Following the taste panel rules, Anna waited until the other kids had taken a bite before saying, "That's a good snack that I made." John agreed, saying he liked the way the waffle holes "get filled up with good stuff."

Sleeping Pickle

Pictured on page 23.

2 slices bread **Butter *or* margarine**	● Spread one side of the bread slices with butter or margarine. Place on an ungreased baking sheet.
2 slices boiled ham *or* any **square luncheon meat**	● Place a meat slice atop each slice of buttered bread.
1 whole dill *or* sweet pickle, **cut in half lengthwise**	● Place a pickle half atop each slice of meat on the bread.
2 slices American *or* brick **cheese**	● Top each with a cheese slice, covering all but one end of the pickle. (If desired, fold back one corner of the cheese.) Bake in a 400° oven for 7 to 8 minutes or till edges of bread are crisp and cheese is melted. Makes 2.

Cover the pickle with a blanket of cheese so its "head" pokes out from under the covers. Let the pickle nap in the oven until the cheese melts and the bread bed is toasty on the edges.

Two-Tone Juice

EQUIPMENT
glass measuring cup   small glass

¼ cup chilled peach nectar
¼ cup chilled red Hawaiian
   fruit punch drink *or*
   cherry drink

● Pour peach nectar into a small glass. Tilt the glass and slowly add the red fruit drink, as shown below. Do not stir. Makes 1 serving.

This drink stays in two layers because the juice on the bottom is heavier than the juice on top.

To make the two layers, first pour in the peach nectar. Then tilt the glass a little bit and slowly pour the red fruit drink down the side of the glass so that the red drink floats on top of the nectar.

Peanut Butter Mustache-Maker

1 cup milk

● In a saucepan heat milk till tiny bubbles form around the edges but *do not boil.* Pour into a blender container.

Take a sip of this warm, creamy drink, and you'll see why we call it a mustache-maker.

2 tablespoons creamy
   peanut butter
1 teaspoon honey
2 large marshmallows
   (optional)

● Add peanut butter and honey. Cover and blend till smooth.
   Pour into two coffee cups or teacups. If desired, top each with a marshmallow. Makes 2 (5-ounce) servings.

MICROWAVE TIMING
In a 2-cup glass measure, micro-cook milk on HIGH (100%) power for 2 to 2½ minutes or till very hot; *do not boil.* Continue as directed in the recipe.

Pink Punch

1 tablespoon frozen pineapple juice concentrate 1 tablespoon frozen cranberry juice concentrate	● Place frozen pineapple juice concentrate and frozen cranberry juice concentrate in an 8-ounce glass.	**Make a *Fruit Kabob* stirrer using one or more kinds of fruit. On a plastic toothpick or cocktail straw, thread bite-size pieces of fruit such as strawberries, pineapple chunks, maraschino cherries, orange sections, or seedless grapes.**
Ginger ale *or* lemon-lime carbonated beverage Ice cubes Fruit Kabob (see tip, right)	● Pour ginger ale or lemon-lime carbonated beverage into the glass till *three-fourths* full; stir. Add 2 or 3 ice cubes and a Fruit Kabob. Makes 1.	

Orange Fizz Float

EQUIPMENT ice cream scoop spoon 8-ounce glass		**You don't have to measure anything to make this float.**
Vanilla ice cream	● Drop a scoop of ice cream into an 8-ounce glass.	
Orange juice Lemon-lime carbonated beverage	● Fill the glass *three-fourths* full with orange juice. Pour in enough lemon-lime beverage to fill the glass. Give it a stir with a spoon. Makes 1 serving.	

Cinnamon Sippin' Cider

3 cups apple cider *or* apple juice 1 cup cranberry juice cocktail 8 inches stick cinnamon, broken	● In a saucepan combine apple cider or apple juice, cranberry juice cocktail, and stick cinnamon. Bring to boiling; reduce heat. Simmer, uncovered, for 5 minutes. Remove stick cinnamon. Serve warm or chilled. Makes 4 (8-ounce) servings.	**MICROWAVE TIMING** In a 2-quart nonmetal casserole combine apple cider or juice and cranberry juice cocktail. Stir in ¼ teaspoon *ground cinnamon* instead of the stick cinnamon. Micro-cook on HIGH (100%) power, uncovered, about 10 minutes or till mixture begins to boil.

Creamy Coolers

Also pictured on the cover.

½ cup sugar
1 envelope *unsweetened*
    soft drink mix
    (any flavor)

● Stir together sugar and fruit-flavored drink mix; store in a tightly covered container till ready to use.

Wow! Pink lemonade, lemon-lime, grape, orange, black cherry, strawberry, raspberry, lemonade . . . pick your favorite fruit flavor and make a shake.

Milk
Vanilla ice cream

● For 1 serving, in a blender container combine *1 cup* of milk, *1 small scoop* of vanilla ice cream, and *1 to 2 tablespoons* of the soft drink mixture. Cover and blend till smooth. Pour into a glass. Makes 1 (12-ounce) serving.

For 4 to 6 servings, in a blender container combine *2 cups* of milk, *4 to 6 small scoops* of vanilla ice cream, and *⅓ to ½ cup* of the soft drink mixture. Cover and blend till smooth. Stir in *2 cups* more milk. Pour into glasses. Makes 4 to 6 (12-ounce) servings.

Strawberries Through a Straw

3 cups frozen unsweetened strawberries 1½ cups unsweetened pineapple juice 2 tablespoons honey (optional)	● In a blender container combine frozen strawberries, pineapple juice, and honey, if desired. Cover and blend till smooth. Makes 4 (6-ounce) servings.	**Sipping strawberries through a straw is hard to do, unless you spin them in a blender with some fruit juice. If you like, sweeten this 100% natural drink with a little honey.**

Chocolate-Peanut-Banana Swirl

1 medium banana	● Cut the banana into 1-inch pieces. Wrap pieces in foil and freeze.	**It looks like a chocolate milk shake but your taste buds will tell you it's much, much more.** Freeze the banana before blending the shake to make every sip refreshingly cold.
1 cup milk 1 cup chocolate ice cream ¼ cup creamy peanut butter	● Unwrap the banana pieces. In a blender container combine banana, milk, chocolate ice cream, and peanut butter. Cover and blend till smooth. Makes 3 (6-ounce) servings.	

Push-Button Peach Cream

1 cup frozen unsweetened peach slices* *or* one 8¾-ounce can peach slices, chilled and drained ½ of an 8-ounce carton (½ cup) vanilla yogurt ¼ cup milk ⅛ teaspoon ground nutmeg	● In a blender container combine frozen or canned peach slices, vanilla yogurt, milk, and ⅛ teaspoon nutmeg. Cover the blender container; blend till the mixture is smooth.	**With the push of a button on an electric blender, you can turn peaches and yogurt into a thick and creamy shake.**
Ground nutmeg	● Pour into two small glasses. Sprinkle each with a little more nutmeg. Makes 2 (4-ounce) servings. ***Note:** If you use frozen peach slices, add 1 tablespoon *honey* to the mixture before blending.	

Mint-Chocolate Moo

1 pint chocolate ice cream
1 cup milk
1 teaspoon vanilla
¼ teaspoon peppermint
   extract

● In a blender container combine the chocolate ice cream, milk, vanilla, and peppermint extract. Cover the blender container; blend till the mixture is smooth. Makes 4 (6-ounce) servings.

The best description of this drink comes from our junior testers who say it tastes like chocolate-covered mints.

Cow in the Apple Orchard

1¾ cups milk
½ of a 6-ounce can (⅓ cup)
   frozen apple juice
   concentrate

● In a blender container combine milk and apple juice concentrate. Cover and blend till well mixed.

1 cup vanilla ice cream
½ teaspoon ground
   cinnamon

● Add vanilla ice cream and cinnamon; cover and blend till smooth. Makes 5 (6-ounce) servings.

Do you know why this recipe has such a silly name? Our group of young tasters have the answer. "It smells and tastes like apples, and the cow made the milk!"

Frutti-Tutti Milk Shakes

1¼ cups cold milk
1 8¾-ounce can peach
   slices
1 11-ounce can pineapple
   tidbits and mandarin
   orange sections, drained
1 cup ice cubes
½ cup cream-style cottage
   cheese

● Pour milk into a blender container. Drain peach slices, reserving 1 tablespoon of the syrup.

   Add reserved syrup, peach slices, pineapple tidbits and mandarin orange sections, half of the ice cubes, and the cottage cheese to the blender container. Cover and blend well.

   Add the remaining ice cubes; cover and blend till mixture is smooth. Makes 5 (6-ounce) servings.

Frutti-Tutti Freezer Pops: Prepare *Frutti-Tutti Milk Shakes* as at left, *except* pour into five 7-ounce paper cups. Cover each with foil. Make a small hole in the foil with a knife. Insert a wooden stick into cup through hole. (See tip on page 38 for Freezing Pops on Sticks.) Freeze 6 hours or till firm. Before serving, let stand 5 minutes. Remove foil and paper.

Frozen Fruit

For a fresh and different snack, try a piece of frozen fruit. It's easy to fix and nutritious too. Small fruits such as cherries, grapes, and pineapple chunks are ready to freeze. Peel and slice bananas, peaches, and pears and coat them with lemon juice. For melon, scoop out balls with a melon ball cutter. Peel and section oranges.

Put the fruit in a single layer in a freezer container. (If you want to, stick a toothpick in each piece of fruit before freezing. Or thread several pieces on a wooden skewer.) Cover and freeze. When snack time rolls around, pull out the frozen fruit and enjoy!

Hide-and-Seek Fruit

EQUIPMENT

small mixing bowl	fork or spoon
measuring cups	3 cereal bowls
measuring spoons	large spoon

1 4½- *or* 5-ounce can vanilla pudding
¼ cup orange yogurt
3 tablespoons milk

● In a small mixing bowl stir together vanilla pudding, orange yogurt, and milk with a fork or spoon.

¾ cup bite-size fruit pieces such as strawberries, grapes, orange sections, *or* pineapple chunks

● Divide the fruit between three cereal bowls. Spoon *one-third* of the pudding mixture over the fruit in each bowl. Makes 3 servings.

"Yummy pudding stuff" is what taste-testing kids called the topping that covers the fruit. Pick the fruit that you like the best and hide it under the "yummy pudding stuff" that you make.

Banana Tree Stumps

Pictured on page 35.

¼ cup butterscotch pieces 1 tablespoon peanut butter	● In a small saucepan, combine the butterscotch pieces and peanut butter. Cook over low heat, stirring constantly, till butterscotch pieces are melted. Remove from heat.
1 medium banana	● Peel the banana. With a knife, cut the banana into 1-inch pieces.
½ cup finely chopped peanuts *or* almond brickle pieces	● Dip each piece of banana into the butterscotch mixture. Lift out with a fork. Roll in the chopped peanuts or almond brickle pieces to coat. Place on a waxed-paper-lined plate. Chill 2 hours. Serves 2.

"Crunchy!" "Yummy!" "Good!" are the comments we heard from kids tasting these peanut-coated banana chunks. Because the pieces are bite-size, the kids agreed they could each eat four or five.

Apple-Cherry Bombs

1 medium cooking apple	● Core apple. Peel off a strip around top of apple. Place apple in a 10-ounce custard cup or casserole.
3 *or* 4 maraschino cherries 1 teaspoon butter *or* margarine	● Place cherries into hole of apple. Place butter or margarine atop apple over the hole.
¼ cup black-cherry-flavored carbonated beverage *or* apple juice	● Pour carbonated beverage or apple juice over apple. Bake in a 350° oven about 45 minutes or till apple is tender.
Granola	● Serve warm or chilled. Sprinkle apple with granola before serving. Serves 1.

This juicy apple bomb is loaded with red cherries that will set off a flavorful explosion in your mouth.

MICROWAVE TIMING
Core and peel apple as directed. Place in a 10-ounce custard cup or nonmetal casserole. Fill with cherries; top with butter. Pour carbonated beverage or juice over apple. Micro-cook on HIGH (100%) power 2 to 3 minutes or till tender. Top with granola.

Dive-In Fruit Dip

EQUIPMENT

measuring cups	small bowl
colander	spoon
table knife, if needed	

First get the fruit ready to take a swim. Then mix the creamy "pool" using your favorite fruit yogurt and whipped dessert topping. Now, dive in!

¼ cup frozen whipped dessert topping

● Take the dessert topping out of the freezer. Let it stand on the counter while you get the fruit ready.

1 cup fresh fruit such as strawberries, grapes, *or* cherries, *or* 1 medium orange, banana, apple, pear, *or* peach

● For strawberries, grapes, or cherries, put the fruit in a colander. Put the colander in the sink and run cold water over the fruit to wash it. For an orange, peel it and pull apart the sections. For a banana, peel it and cut it into chunks with a table knife. For an apple, pear, or peach, have an adult slice it for you.

½ of an 8-ounce carton fruit yogurt

● For dip, in a small bowl use a spoon to stir together yogurt and ¼ cup of softened dessert topping till smooth. To eat, dunk the fruit into the dip. Serves 2.

Apple-Berry Crunch

1 tablespoon red raspberry preserves
1 tablespoon water
Dash ground cinnamon
1 small apple, cored, peeled, and sliced

● In a bowl stir together preserves, water, and cinnamon. Add apple slices; stir to coat.
  Turn mixture into an ungreased 10-ounce custard cup or casserole.

2 tablespoons granola

● Sprinkle the top with granola. Bake in a 350° oven for 20 to 25 minutes or till apple is tender. Serve warm or chilled. Makes 1 serving.

Our taste panel of kids really liked this granola-topped apple snack. It reminded many of them of apple crisp, and they particularly "liked the crunchy on top of the apples."

Apple Smiles

1 red medium apple, cored and sliced
Peanut butter

● Spread one side of each apple slice with peanut butter.

Tiny marshmallows

● Place three or four tiny marshmallows on top of the peanut butter on one apple slice. Top with another apple slice, peanut butter side down. Squeeze gently. Eat right away. Makes 8 to 10.

"It looks like a smile, but the teeth fall out!" said one little taster as she bit into one of the *Apple Smiles* and a tiny marshmallow tumbled out. To make sure the "teeth" stay in, use plenty of peanut butter to stick them to the apple "lips."

Apple Smiles

Curly Taco Mix
(see recipe, page 13)

Banana Tree Stumps
(see recipe, page 33)

Pinecones

1 8-ounce can pineapple tidbits (juice pack)	● Drain the juice from the pineapple. (Save the juice for drinking.) Place the pineapple in a small mixing bowl.
1 4½- or 5-ounce can vanilla pudding	● Add vanilla pudding. Stir to mix well.
3 ice-cream cones Granola	● Spoon *one-third* of the mixture into *each* ice-cream cone. Sprinkle granola on top. Serve right away. Makes 3.

Frozen Pinecones: Prepare Pinecones as above, *except* set filled cones upright in paper cups. Freeze 4 to 6 hours or till firm. For longer freezing, cover with moisture- and vaporproof wrap. Let stand at room temperature 5 minutes before serving.

These *Pinecones* don't grow on trees. You make them by filling ice-cream cones with pineapple pudding and topping them off with granola.

If you like, make them into a frosty snack by sticking them in the freezer until firm.

Unpeeled Banana Split

1 small banana	● With a sharp knife slit the peel of the banana lengthwise, but *do not* remove the peel or cut through the fruit inside. Place the unpeeled banana in a dish. Pull back the peel from the fruit, as shown below.
1 teaspoon strawberry jam Chocolate-flavored syrup *or* miniature semisweet chocolate pieces **1 teaspoon pineapple preserves** **Chopped nuts (optional)**	● Spoon strawberry jam, chocolate-flavored syrup or chocolate pieces, and pineapple preserves onto different sections of the banana. If desired, sprinkle chopped nuts over all. Serves 1.

There are two silly things about this banana split. One is that it doesn't have any ice cream! The other you can guess from the title. (You eat this banana right out of its skin.)

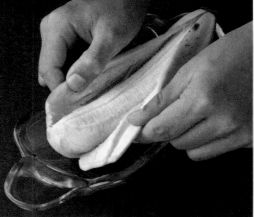

After the banana peel has been slit, kids can pull back the peel from the fruit to make room for spooning in the goodies.

Pizza in a Cup

1 single-serving envelope
   instant tomato soup mix
⅛ teaspoon dried oregano,
   crushed

● Prepare tomato soup mix according to package directions, *except* stir in oregano with the dry soup mix.

With just a few additions, we turned plain tomato soup into a pizzalike treat that brought these compliments from kids: "It's good!" "Tastes like pizza!" "I like it!"

2 tablespoons chopped
   pepperoni *or* salami
2 tablespoons shredded
   mozzarella cheese *or*
   cheddar cheese
1 to 2 tablespoons herb-
   seasoned croutons

● Stir in chopped pepperoni or salami and shredded cheese. Top soup with croutons. Makes 1 serving.

Rumpelstilt-Skins

1 medium potato, baked

● Cut potato lengthwise into quarters. Scoop out potato, leaving skins ¼ inch thick. (Save scooped-out potato for another use.) Place potato skins on a baking sheet.

Just as Rumpelstiltskin of fairy-tale fame turned straw into gold, you can turn leftovers into a great snack for kids.

2 teaspoons cooked bacon
   pieces, finely chopped
   fully cooked ham, finely
   chopped cooked turkey,
   or flaked tuna
1 teaspoon shredded
   cheddar cheese *and/or*
   French-fried onions,
   slightly crushed

● Sprinkle potato skins with bacon, ham, turkey, or tuna. Top with cheese or crushed French-fried onions or both.
   Bake in a 350° oven about 5 minutes or till hot. Makes 2 servings.

MICROWAVE TIMING
Place the potato skins on a nonmetal plate. Sprinkle with meat, cheese, and/or French-fried onions. Micro-cook on HIGH (100%) power for 15 to 30 seconds or till hot.

Soda Pop Pops

2 12-ounce cans (3 cups)
  lemon-lime carbonated
  beverage
1 14-ounce can (1¼ cups)
  sweetened condensed
  milk
¼ cup lemon juice
10 wooden sticks

● In a bowl stir together carbonated beverage, sweetened condensed milk, and lemon juice.

Pour into ten 5-ounce paper cups. Cover each cup with foil. Make a small hole in the foil with a knife. Insert a wooden stick into the cup through the hole. Freeze 4 to 6 hours or till firm.

To serve, remove foil and tear off paper. Makes 10.

Food editors and kids agreed that these pops are tops. The editors' comments, such as "creamy" and "not overly sweet," are no match for the description of a child: "It tastes like a frozen ice-cream soda!"

Freezing Pops on Sticks

Pour the mixture to be frozen into paper or plastic cups. Cover each with foil. Make a small hole in the foil with the tip of a knife. (To make cutting the hole easier, hold down the edges of the foil with one hand.)

Slip a wooden stick through the hole till the stick almost touches the bottom of the cup. Put cups in the freezer so they're level. Freeze till firm. To serve, remove foil. Peel off paper or remove from plastic cup.

Granola Burr-r-r Ball

EQUIPMENT

measuring cup	1 freezer-proof
medium bowl	dessert dish
ice cream scoop	

Do you wonder why this snack has such a funny name? One reason is the granola looks like a cluster of prickly burrs— the kind that sometimes cling to your socks when you run through tall grass. Another is that the ice cream on the inside is so cold, you'll shiver and say "burr-r-r."

¼ cup granola 1 scoop ice cream	● Put granola in a medium bowl. Break up any big pieces with your fingers. Drop the scoop of ice cream into the granola. With your hands roll the ice cream in the granola, shaping it into a ball and pressing granola into the sides. Place in a freezer-proof dish. Freeze till firm.
Honey (if you like)	● If you like, drizzle the ice cream with honey before you eat it. Makes 1 serving.

Alaska Sandwiches

½ cup vanilla yogurt ¼ cup sifted powdered sugar ¼ cup chopped peanuts ¼ cup peanut butter	● For filling, in a small mixing bowl stir together vanilla yogurt, powdered sugar, chopped peanuts, and peanut butter till well mixed.
24 to 28 chocolate chip, peanut butter, *or* oatmeal cookies (2 to 2½ inches in diameter)	● On the flat side of one cookie spread filling ½ inch thick, spreading almost to edge. Top with another cookie, flat side down. Press cookies together gently so filling is even with edge. Repeat with remaining cookies and filling. 　Wrap individually in moisture- and vaporproof wrap. Freeze several hours or till firm. Makes 12 to 14.

They look like little ice cream sandwiches, but with yogurt and peanut butter in them, they're a much wiser treat. Keep a batch in the freezer for an already-ready snack.

Flash Cubes

Pictured on page 41.

¼ cup sugar 1 envelope unflavored gelatin 1½ cups water 1 6-ounce can frozen apple juice concentrate	● In a medium saucepan stir together sugar and unflavored gelatin. Stir in water and apple juice concentrate. Heat and stir about 5 minutes or till the concentrate is melted and the sugar and gelatin are dissolved.
½ cup orange juice ¼ cup lemon juice 28 wooden sticks	● Stir in orange juice and lemon juice. Pour into two plastic ice cube trays (14 cubes each). Cover with foil and freeze 3 hours or till partially frozen. 　Remove foil. Insert a wooden stick into each cube. Freeze overnight or till firm. To serve, loosen edges of cubes with a knife. Pop out cubes. Makes 28.

Flash Cubes like these aren't good for taking pictures, but they are good to eat and good for you. They're made with fruit juices and gelatin mixed together in a flash. To eat, just pop them out of the ice cube trays and start licking.

Yogie Pear Pops

1 **16-ounce can pear halves**
 ***or* slices, drained**
1 **8-ounce carton plain**
 yogurt
3 **tablespoons honey**
½ **teaspoon lemon juice**
 Few drops almond extract
 (optional)

● In a blender container or food processor bowl combine pears, yogurt, honey, lemon juice, and almond extract, if desired. Cover and blend or process till smooth. Pour the mixture into five 5-ounce paper cups.

Before we told our junior tasters the name of these pops, they couldn't tell what flavors they were tasting. All they knew was that they liked them. But when we told the kids they're called *Yogie Pear Pops*, they guessed right off the bat what they were eating—yogurt and pears.

5 **wooden sticks**

● Cover each cup with foil. Make a small hole in the foil with a knife. Insert a wooden stick into the cup through the hole. Freeze 4 to 6 hours or till firm.
 To serve, remove foil and tear paper from pops. Makes 5 servings.

Pictured, left to right:
Yogie Pear Pops
Peachy Keen Pops
(see recipe, page 43)
Three-Fruit Pops
Florida Freezer Pops
(see recipe, page 43)
Flash Cubes
(see recipe, page 39)
Apple Pie Pops
(see recipe, page 42)

Three-Fruit Pops

½ cup orange juice
1 red medium apple,
  quartered and cored
1 medium orange, peeled
  and sectioned
1 small banana, peeled and
  cut up

● In a blender container or food processor bowl combine orange juice, apple, orange, and banana. Cover and blend or process till smooth. Pour into six 3-ounce paper cups.

Once upon a time there was an orange, an apple, a banana, and some orange juice that got mixed up together in a blender . . . This story has a happy ending because kids like the fruity flavor of these pops and grown-ups know they're giving their kids a healthy snack.

6 wooden sticks

● Cover each cup with foil. Make a small hole in the foil with a knife. Insert a wooden stick into the cup through the hole. Freeze 4 to 6 hours or till firm.

Remove from freezer 10 minutes before serving. Remove foil and tear paper from pops. Makes 6 servings.

To make bar-shape pops, freeze the fruit mixture in plastic freezer-pop molds.

Peanut Butter Lick-Sticks

1 **pint vanilla ice cream, softened**	● In a mixer bowl combine ice cream and peanut butter. Beat with an electric mixer on medium speed till well mixed.
½ **cup peanut butter**	

¼ **cup granola** *or* **4 teaspoons of your favorite jam**
4 **wooden sticks**

● Pour *half* of the ice cream mixture into four 7-ounce paper cups. Spoon *1 tablespoon* granola or *1 teaspoon* jam over ice cream mixture in each cup. Top with remaining ice cream mixture.

Cover each cup with foil. Make a small hole in the foil with a knife. Insert a wooden stick into the cup through the hole. Freeze about 4 hours or till firm.

To serve, remove foil and tear off paper. Makes 4.

If your kids like peanut butter and they like ice cream too, they can't help but like this lickable snack. Our little tasters told us that the pops with granola in the middle tasted like peanut butter cookies and ice cream. The pops with jam in the middle reminded them of peanut butter and jelly sandwiches.

Apple Pie Pops

Pictured on page 41.

EQUIPMENT

small mixing bowl	3- or 5-ounce
measuring cup	paper cups
measuring spoons	foil
spoon	table knife
waxed paper	4 wooden sticks

½ **cup plain yogurt**
½ **cup applesauce**
2 **tablespoons honey**

● In a small mixing bowl use a spoon to stir together yogurt, applesauce, and honey till well mixed.

2 **oatmeal cookies**
4 **wooden sticks**

● Put a piece of waxed paper on the table or counter. Holding the cookies over the waxed paper, crumble the cookies into small pieces with your fingers. Pour the crumbled cookies into the mixture in the bowl. Stir to mix well.

Spoon into four 3- or 5-ounce paper cups. Cover each cup with foil. Holding the foil around the side of the cup with one hand, use a table knife in your other hand to make a small hole in the foil. Put a wooden stick into the cup through the hole. Freeze 3 to 4 hours or till firm.

To eat, take off the foil and tear the paper off the pop. Makes 4.

"It sort of tastes like apple pie," said one of our kid taste-testers. "The cookie in there is like the crust of the pie."

When eight-year-old Sarah made these pops, she came up with this handy tip: Put one paper cup inside another before filling so the cups will be sturdier for covering and carrying to the freezer.

Peachy Keen Pops

Pictured on page 40.

½ cup drained canned peach slices ¼ cup orange juice	● In a blender container combine peaches and orange juice. Cover and blend till smooth.
1 cup raspberry sherbet 5 wooden sticks	● Add sherbet a spoonful at a time through opening in lid, blending till smooth after each addition. 　Pour into five 3-ounce paper cups. Cover each cup with foil. Make a small hole in the foil with a knife. Insert a wooden stick into the cup through the hole. Freeze 4 to 6 hours or till firm. 　To serve, remove foil and tear off paper. Makes 5.

These colorful pops were the favorite of several little tasters. One child thought they would be good for a birthday party. Another, thinking he'd like them more often, chimed in, "They would be good on almost any kind of summer day."

Florida Freezer Pops

Pictured on page 41.

1 12-ounce can (1½ cups) evaporated milk	● Pour evaporated milk into an 8x4x2-inch loaf pan. Freeze for 1½ to 2 hours or till ice crystals form around edges. 　Transfer the icy mixture to a large mixer bowl. Beat with an electric mixer on medium speed till soft peaks form.
1 14-ounce can (1¼ cups) *sweetened condensed milk* 1 12-ounce can frozen orange juice concentrate, thawed ¼ cup nonfat dry milk powder 14 wooden sticks	● Gradually beat in the sweetened condensed milk, orange juice concentrate, and nonfat dry milk powder. Beat for 2 to 3 minutes or till fluffy. 　Pour ½ cup into *each* 5-ounce paper cup. Cover each cup with foil. Make a small hole in the foil with a knife. Insert a wooden stick into the cup through the hole. Freeze overnight or till firm.
Toasted *or* tinted coconut, granola, chopped nuts, *or* crushed graham crackers (optional)	● To serve, remove foil and tear off paper. If desired, after standing at room temperature for 5 minutes, dip tops of pops into toasted or tinted coconut, granola, chopped nuts, or crushed graham crackers. Makes 14 servings.

These creamy orange freezer treats will remind you of the delicious frozen bars you can buy that combine orange sherbet and vanilla ice cream.

Ice Scraper

EQUIPMENT
small bowl	measuring spoons
can opener or	spoon
measuring cup	clear plastic wrap

1 **8½-ounce can (1 cup) applesauce**
1 **tablespoon brown sugar**
2 **teaspoons lemon juice**
¼ **teaspoon vanilla**

● In a small bowl use a spoon to stir together applesauce, brown sugar, lemon juice, and vanilla. Cover with clear plastic wrap; freeze at least 5 hours.

Before serving, take the bowl out of the freezer and let stand 5 minutes. Scrape across top with a spoon (the picture below shows you how) and put in dishes. Makes 3 servings.

Note: To make frozen pops, spoon the applesauce mixture into three 3-ounce paper cups. Cover each with foil. Make a small hole in the foil with a table knife. Slip a wooden stick into the hole. Freeze. To eat, take off the foil and paper.

Ryan and Sonya are two of the kids who tried this frozen treat for us. "It tastes like applesauce," Ryan said. "And ice cubes," added Sonya.

Let the bowl of frozen applesauce stand on the counter for 5 minutes to soften a little bit. Then scrape across the top with a spoon. Put the shavings in a dish and enjoy a cool, delicious snack.

Cookie Crumb Ice Cream

Pictured on page 4.

2 **cups whipping cream**
½ **of a 14-ounce can (⅔ cup) sweetened condensed milk**
½ **teaspoon vanilla**

● In a large mixer bowl combine whipping cream, sweetened condensed milk, and vanilla. Chill for 30 minutes.

Beat with an electric mixer on high speed till soft peaks form.

12 **chocolate sandwich cookies**

● Coarsely crumble the cookies; fold into the cream mixture. Transfer to an 8x8x2-inch pan. Cover and freeze about 4 hours or till firm.

To serve, scoop out with an ice cream scoop. Makes about 1 quart.

Many of the little tykes who tasted the recipes in this book told us that cookies and ice cream are their favorite snacks. Both favorites together in this recipe got high marks from the kids—and from those grown-ups lucky enough to get a taste.

Sure-Bet Sherbetwiches

¾ cup desired sherbet
One 6-ounce can

● Spoon sherbet into a clean 6-ounce can. Cover the open end with foil; freeze at least 2 hours or till firm.

16 butter-flavored cookies *or* other small round cookies

● Remove foil and other end of can. Press on one end, forcing sherbet out. With a sharp knife cut the sherbet into eight slices about ½ inch thick.

Place a sherbet slice on the flat side of one cookie. Top with another cookie, flat side down. Repeat with remaining sherbet and cookies. Serve at once or refreeze in a shallow pan. Makes 8.

To assemble the sherbet-wiches, push the sherbet through the can and cut into ½-inch slices.

Put a sherbet slice on the flat side of one cookie. Top with another cookie, flat side down.

Rise-and-Shine Raisin Bran Muffins

½ of a 15-ounce box (4 cups) raisin bran cereal
2½ cups all-purpose flour
1 cup sugar
½ cup chopped walnuts
2½ teaspoons baking soda
1 teaspoon salt

● In a large mixing bowl stir together raisin bran cereal, flour, sugar, chopped walnuts, baking soda, and salt. Make a well in the center.

2 beaten eggs
2 cups buttermilk
½ cup cooking oil

● In another bowl beat together eggs, buttermilk, and oil. Add to the flour mixture, stirring just till moistened (batter will be thick). Cover and store in the refrigerator up to 3 weeks.

● To bake muffins, spoon batter into greased or paper-bake-cup-lined muffin cups, filling three-fourths full. Bake in a 375° oven for 20 to 25 minutes. Remove from pans. Serve warm. Makes enough batter for 24 muffins.

Kids told us they would eat these bran muffins morning, afternoon, and evening. The batter keeps in the refrigerator for up to 3 weeks so the muffins will be ready to go when you are.

Yo-Yo Muffins

1 cup all-purpose flour
1 cup whole wheat flour
2 teaspoons baking powder
½ teaspoon salt
¼ teaspoon ground nutmeg

● In a medium mixing bowl stir together all-purpose flour, whole wheat flour, baking powder, salt, and nutmeg. Make a well in the center.

2 slightly beaten eggs
⅓ cup honey
¼ cup cooking oil
1 8-ounce carton orange, lemon, pineapple, peach, *or* spiced apple yogurt

● In another bowl combine eggs, honey, and oil; stir in yogurt. Stir yogurt mixture into the flour mixture just till dry ingredients are moistened.
    Spoon batter into greased muffin cups, filling three-fourths full. Bake in a 400° oven for 18 to 20 minutes or till golden. Remove from pans. Serve warm. Makes 12.

Yo-Yo Muffins **are named for their star ingredient— yogurt. Though you may not taste the yogurt itself, it's hard at work making the muffins moist and lending its fruity flavor.**

MICROWAVE WARM-UP To reheat in the microwave oven, place one muffin on a nonmetal plate. Micro-cook on HIGH (100%) power for 8 seconds.

Blue-Eyed Corn Muffins

¾ cup all-purpose flour
¾ cup yellow cornmeal
¼ cup sugar
2 teaspoons baking powder
⅛ teaspoon salt

1 beaten egg
¾ cup milk
¼ cup cooking oil

¾ cup fresh *or* frozen
blueberries, thawed

● In a medium mixing bowl stir together flour, cornmeal, sugar, baking powder, and salt. Make a well in the center.

● In another bowl combine egg, milk, and oil; add all at once to flour mixture. Stir just till moistened; do not overbeat.

● Fold in the blueberries. Spoon batter into greased muffin cups, filling three-fourths full.
   Bake in a 400° oven for 20 to 25 minutes or till golden. Remove from pans. Serve warm. Makes about 12.

It's hard to turn down a corn muffin with big blueberry eyes begging you to take a bite.

MICROWAVE WARM-UP
To reheat in the microwave oven, place one muffin on a nonmetal plate. Micro-cook on HIGH (100%) power for 8 seconds.

Peanut Butter-Oatmeal Muffins *(see recipe, page 49)*

Rise-and-Shine Raisin Bran Muffins

Gold Mine Muffins
(see recipe, page 49)

Blue-Eyed Corn Muffins

Ugly Dumplings

1 medium peach *or* pear *or* 1 small apple	● Remove and discard pit or core from fruit. Peel and chop fruit.
1 package (10) refrigerated biscuits	● Separate biscuits. On a lightly floured surface pat or roll each into a 4-inch circle. Place about *1 tablespoon* of chopped fruit on *each* biscuit.
2 tablespoons sugar **¼ teaspoon ground cinnamon** **2 tablespoons butter *or* margarine**	● Stir together sugar and cinnamon; sprinkle over fruit. Dot each with some of the 2 tablespoons butter or margarine, as shown below, left.
1 tablespoon butter *or* margarine, melted	● Shape into half-moons or bundles. For half-moons, moisten edge of biscuits; fold in half over filling. Press with your fingers or a fork to seal. Place about 2 inches apart on an ungreased baking sheet, as shown below. For bundles, moisten edge of biscuits; gather edge over filling. Pinch with your fingers to seal. Place in an ungreased muffin pan, as shown below, right. Brush with the 1 tablespoon melted butter or margarine. Bake in a 375° oven for 11 to 13 minutes or till golden. Remove to wire rack. Serve warm. Makes 10 servings.

As in the story of the ugly duckling, this biscuit snack starts out looking funny and turns into something wonderful!

MICROWAVE WARM-UP
To reheat in the microwave oven, place one dumpling on a nonmetal plate. Micro-cook on HIGH (100%) power for 8 seconds.

Before sealing the dumplings, sprinkle the fruit with the sugar-cinnamon mixture and dot with butter.

Shape the dumplings in one of two ways. For half-moons, moisten edge of the biscuit; fold in half over filling. Seal and bake on a baking sheet.

For bundles, moisten edge and gather together over filling. Pinch to seal, and bake in a muffin pan.

Peanut Butter-Oatmeal Muffins

Pictured on page 47.

¾ cup all-purpose flour ¼ cup quick-cooking rolled oats 2 tablespoons toasted wheat germ 1 teaspoon baking powder ¼ teaspoon baking soda ⅛ teaspoon salt	● In a medium mixing bowl stir together the flour, quick-cooking rolled oats, 2 tablespoons wheat germ, baking powder, baking soda, and salt. Make a well in the center of the flour mixture.
⅓ cup packed brown sugar ¼ cup peanut butter 1 egg	● In a small mixer bowl beat brown sugar and peanut butter with electric mixer on medium speed till fluffy. Add egg; beat well.
½ cup milk Toasted wheat germ	● Add the flour mixture and milk alternately to the beaten mixture, beating just till blended after each addition. Grease muffin cups; sprinkle lightly with wheat germ to coat cups. (Or, line muffin cups with paper bake cups.) Spoon batter into muffin cups, filling three-fourths full. Sprinkle with additional wheat germ. Bake in a 400° oven for 15 to 20 minutes or till golden. Remove from pans. Serve warm. Makes about 8.

Kids that taste-tested these muffins said they had the flavor of peanut butter cookies. They also told us that butter and honey or jelly would be good on the muffins.

MICROWAVE WARM-UP
To reheat in the microwave oven, place one muffin on a nonmetal plate. Micro-cook on HIGH (100%) power for 8 seconds.

Gold Mine Muffins

Pictured on page 47.

1 egg ¼ cup milk 1 8¾-ounce can cream-style corn 1 4-ounce package (1 cup) shredded cheddar cheese	● In a medium mixing bowl beat together egg and milk. Mix in cream-style corn and shredded cheddar cheese.
1½ cups packaged pancake mix	● Stir in pancake mix just till moistened. Spoon the batter into greased or paper-bake-cup-lined muffin cups, filling three-fourths full.
½ cup corn chips, crushed (about ¼ cup)	● Sprinkle crushed corn chips on top of the batter; gently press into batter. Bake in a 400° oven for 15 to 20 minutes or till golden and a toothpick inserted in center comes out clean. Remove from pans. Serve warm. Makes about 12.

Crispy corn chips sit on top of these wholesome muffins. When you open them up, you'll "see a lot of stuff," says 10-year-old Jeremy, like gold nuggets of corn and streaks of cheddar cheese.

MICROWAVE WARM-UP
To reheat in the microwave oven, place one muffin on a nonmetal plate. Micro-cook on HIGH (100%) power for 8 seconds.

Hot Curlers

1 2¼-ounce can deviled ham ½ cup shredded Swiss, cheddar, *or* Monterey Jack cheese (2 ounces) ½ teaspoon prepared mustard	● In a small bowl combine the deviled ham, shredded Swiss, cheddar, or Monterey Jack cheese, and prepared mustard. Set aside.
1 package (10) refrigerated biscuits	● Separate biscuits; pat or roll each into a 4-inch circle. Spread *each* circle with about *1 tablespoon* of the ham mixture. Roll up jelly-roll style. Grease muffin pan. Place *two* rolled-up biscuits, side by side, in *each* muffin cup, curving each into a U-shape with the open ends up.
Milk *or* water	● Using a pastry brush or your finger, brush rolls with milk or water. Bake in a 350° oven for 20 to 25 minutes or till golden brown; remove. Serve warm. Wrap and store any remaining in the refrigerator. Makes 5.

Kids, you can help shape *Hot Curlers* before an adult puts them in the oven. Pat the biscuits into circles, roll them up with ham and cheese inside, and brush with milk or water so the crust will turn out crispy and shiny.

MICROWAVE WARM-UP
To reheat in the microwave oven, place one roll on a nonmetal plate. Micro-cook on HIGH (100%) power about 20 seconds or till heated through.

Hay and Gravel Bars

Pictured on page 59.

¼ cup butter *or* margarine 1 cup packed brown sugar	● In a medium saucepan melt the butter or margarine. Remove from heat. Stir in the brown sugar.
1 egg ½ teaspoon vanilla	● Add egg and vanilla; stir to mix well.
1 cup all-purpose flour 1 teaspoon baking powder	● In a small mixing bowl stir together the flour and baking powder. Stir into the mixture in the saucepan.
½ cup coconut ½ cup chopped nuts	● Stir in coconut and nuts. Mix well. Spread the mixture in a greased 11x7x1½-inch baking pan. 　Bake in a 350° oven for 20 to 25 minutes or till a wooden toothpick inserted in center comes out clean. Cool on a wire rack. Cut into bars. Makes 20.

The hay and gravel in these easy bars is really coconut and chopped nuts. The "hay" makes them moist and chewy and the "gravel" gives them flavor and crunch.

Granola Roundups

1 beaten egg ¾ cup cooking oil ½ cup packed brown sugar ½ cup honey ¼ cup water 1 teaspoon salt 1 teaspoon vanilla	● In a small mixing bowl beat together the egg, cooking oil, brown sugar, honey, water, salt, and vanilla with a wooden spoon till well mixed.
3 cups quick-cooking rolled oats 1 cup whole wheat flour ¾ cup toasted wheat germ	● In a large mixing bowl stir together oats, whole wheat flour, and wheat germ. Add the liquid mixture to the flour mixture; mix well.
1 6-ounce package (1 cup) semisweet chocolate pieces, butterscotch pieces, *or* peanut butter-flavored pieces ½ cup sunflower nuts	● Stir in chocolate, butterscotch, or peanut butter-flavored pieces and sunflower nuts. Drop dough from a ¼-cup measure, 2 inches apart, onto greased cookie sheets. Flatten each mound to 3 inches in diameter. 　Bake in a 350° oven for 15 to 20 minutes or till light brown. Remove; cool on a wire rack. Makes about 20 cookies.

Granola bars are a popular snack with the kids we talked to. These hefty, healthy cookies are a lot like granola bars, except for one thing. They're round!

Flannel Jammies

Pictured on page 59.

½ cup butter *or* margarine	● In a mixer bowl beat the butter or margarine with electric mixer on medium speed about 30 seconds or till softened.
3 tablespoons of your favorite jam 1 tablespoon powdered sugar	● Add jam and 1 tablespoon powdered sugar. Beat well.
1 cup all-purpose flour 1 tablespoon toasted wheat germ	● Beat in flour and wheat germ. Shape the dough into 1-inch balls. Place 1 inch apart on an ungreased cookie sheet. Bake in a 325° oven about 20 minutes or till done. Remove; cool thoroughly on a wire rack.
¼ cup sifted powdered sugar	● In a plastic bag place ¼ cup sifted powdered sugar. Shake a few cookies at a time in the powdered sugar till coated. Makes about 24 cookies.

Use your favorite kind of jam to make *Flannel Jammies*. After the cookies are baked and cooled, shake them in a bag with powdered sugar to make them look fuzzy like flannel.

Peanut Butter-Granola Cookies

⅓ cup peanut butter ¼ cup butter *or* margarine ½ cup packed brown sugar	● In a small mixer bowl beat peanut butter and butter or margarine with an electric mixer on medium speed about 30 seconds or till softened. Add brown sugar and beat till fluffy.
1 egg 1 tablespoon milk	● Add egg and milk. Beat well.
½ cup whole wheat flour ¼ teaspoon baking soda	● In a mixing bowl stir together whole wheat flour and baking soda. With mixer on low speed gradually add the flour mixture to the peanut butter mixture, beating till well mixed.
¾ cup granola	● With a wooden spoon stir in granola. Drop dough by rounded teaspoons about 2 inches apart onto ungreased cookie sheets. Bake in a 375° oven for 8 to 10 minutes or till golden. Remove; cool on a wire rack. Makes about 30 cookies.

They look like peanut butter cookies. They taste like peanut butter cookies. They *are* peanut butter cookies, with the extra goodness of granola and whole wheat flour.

Presto-Chango Cookies and Muffins

½ cup butter *or* margarine ¾ cup packed brown sugar	● Beat butter or margarine with electric mixer about 30 seconds or till softened. Add brown sugar; beat till fluffy.
1 egg ½ cup canned pumpkin	● Beat in egg and pumpkin.
¾ cup all-purpose flour ½ teaspoon baking soda ½ teaspoon baking powder ½ teaspoon ground cinnamon ¼ teaspoon salt	● In a mixing bowl stir together flour, baking soda, baking powder, cinnamon, and salt. With mixer on low speed gradually add flour mixture to pumpkin mixture, beating till well mixed.
1½ cups quick-cooking rolled oats	● Stir in oats. Place half (1½ cups) of the dough in another bowl and set aside.
Sesame seed (optional)	● For cookies, drop remaining dough by tablespoons 2 inches apart onto greased cookie sheets. Sprinkle with sesame seed, if desired. Bake in a 375° oven 10 to 12 minutes or till the edges are firm and bottoms are golden. Cool on a wire rack.
3 tablespoons milk Sesame seed (optional)	● For muffins, stir milk into reserved half of dough. Spoon batter into greased or paper-bake-cup-lined muffin cups, filling half full. Sprinkle with sesame seed, if desired. Bake in a 375° oven for 15 to 18 minutes or till a wooden toothpick inserted in center comes out clean. Remove; cool on a wire rack. Makes about 18 cookies *and* 8 muffins.

Ladies and gentlemen, you are about to see cookie dough magically turn into not only a batch of cookies, but a batch of muffins as well. How is it possible, you ask? Read the recipe and find out the secret.

Pucker Bars

Pictured on page 59.

3 cups crisp rice cereal	● Crush the rice cereal to make ¾ cup fine crumbs.
½ cup all-purpose flour 1 tablespoon brown sugar ⅓ cup butter *or* margarine	● For crust, stir together crumbs, the ½ cup flour, and brown sugar. Cut in butter or margarine till well blended. Press crumb mixture onto the bottom of an ungreased 8x8x2-inch baking pan. Bake in a 350° oven for 15 minutes.
3 eggs ⅔ cup sugar 1 teaspoon finely shredded lemon peel ¼ cup lemon juice 1 tablespoon all-purpose flour ½ teaspoon baking powder	● In a small mixing bowl beat together eggs, sugar, lemon peel, lemon juice, 1 tablespoon flour, and the baking powder. Pour over the hot crust. Bake in the 350° oven for 12 to 15 minutes more or till the center is set. Cool in the pan on a wire rack.
Powdered sugar	● Sprinkle with powdered sugar. Cut into squares. Makes 16.

These bars have a tart yet sweet lemony layer on top of a crispy cereal crust.

An easy and tidy way to crush the cereal is to put it in a plastic bag, close the bag, and crush the cereal with your hands.

Polka-Dot Bars

Pictured on page 4.

⅔ cup all-purpose flour ⅓ cup quick-cooking rolled oats 1 teaspoon baking powder ⅛ teaspoon salt	● In a bowl stir together flour, oats, baking powder, and salt. Set aside.
¼ cup butter *or* margarine ¾ cup packed brown sugar	● In a medium saucepan melt butter or margarine; remove from heat. Stir in brown sugar.
1 egg ¼ teaspoon almond extract	● Add egg and almond extract; beat till well combined.
18 pecan halves, walnut halves, maraschino cherry halves, milk chocolate kisses, *or* a combination	● Stir in flour mixture till well mixed. Spread batter in a greased 11x7x1½-inch baking pan. Making 3 long rows of 6 each, place nut halves, maraschino cherry halves, or chocolate kisses atop batter, as shown at right. Bake in a 350° oven 18 to 20 minutes or till a wooden toothpick inserted in center comes out clean. Cool in pan on a wire rack. Cut into bars between "polka dots." Makes 18.

Let kids add the polka dots by placing the nuts, cherries, or kisses in rows on top of the batter.

Fudgy "W" Brownies

½ cup shortening	● In a large saucepan melt shortening over low heat. Remove from heat.
1 cup sugar ⅓ cup unsweetened cocoa powder	● Stir in sugar and cocoa powder.
2 eggs ½ teaspoon vanilla	● Add eggs and vanilla. Stir till blended.
⅔ cup whole wheat flour ½ teaspoon baking powder ¼ teaspoon salt ½ cup chopped nuts	● Combine flour, baking powder, and salt. Stir flour mixture and *half* of the nuts into egg mixture. Spread in a greased 8x8x2-inch baking pan. Sprinkle with remaining nuts. Bake in a 350° oven about 25 minutes or till a slight imprint remains after touching lightly. Cool on a wire rack. Cut into bars. Makes 16.

For kids who are turned off by nutritious-sounding foods, we've kept ingredient "W" a secret. (Our tasters never even suspected whole wheat flour in these brownies.) If the kids ask what the "W" means, tell them it stands for "wonderful."

Freckled Cocoa Cookies

Pictured on pages 58 and 59.

½ cup shortening ½ cup packed brown sugar	● In a small mixer bowl beat shortening and brown sugar with an electric mixer on medium speed till fluffy.
1 egg 2 tablespoons milk 1 teaspoon vanilla	● Add egg, milk, and vanilla. Beat well. (Mixture will look curdled.)
1½ cups whole wheat flour ⅔ cup presweetened cocoa powder ½ teaspoon baking soda ½ teaspoon ground cinnamon ¼ teaspoon salt	● In a medium mixing bowl stir together whole wheat flour, presweetened cocoa powder, baking soda, cinnamon, and salt. With mixer on low speed gradually add flour mixture to shortening mixture, beating till well mixed.
⅓ cup toasted wheat germ	● Drop by rounded teaspoons 2 inches apart onto ungreased cookie sheets. Flatten the dough with the bottom of a drinking glass that has been dipped in wheat germ. Bake in a 350° oven for 8 to 10 minutes or till edges of cookies are firm. Remove from cookie sheets. Cool on a wire rack. Makes about 36 cookies.

Give these cocoa cookies freckles by flattening the dough with the bottom of a glass that has been dipped in wheat germ. For easy dipping, put the wheat germ in a pie plate. The edges of the plate will keep the wheat germ from spreading out too far.

Flying Saucers

Pictured on page 5.

½ cup butter *or* margarine ½ cup sugar ¼ cup packed brown sugar	● In a large mixer bowl beat butter or margarine with electric mixer on medium speed about 30 seconds or till butter is softened. Add sugar and brown sugar; beat till fluffy.
1 egg	● Add the egg. Beat well.
1¼ cups all-purpose flour 1 teaspoon ground cinnamon ½ teaspoon baking soda ½ teaspoon salt	● In a medium mixing bowl stir together flour, cinnamon, baking soda, and salt. With mixer on low speed gradually add flour mixture to butter mixture, beating till well mixed.
½ cup applesauce 1½ cups quick-cooking rolled oats 1 cup small gumdrops, halved	● Beat in applesauce. With a wooden spoon stir in oats and gumdrops. Drop by heaping tablespoons about 3 inches apart onto greased cookie sheets. Bake in a 350° oven about 15 minutes or till golden. Remove; cool on a wire rack. Makes about 20.

These big, soft cookies are called *Flying Saucers* because they look like flying saucers with colored lights.

Chewy Cereal Cookies

½ cup butter *or* margarine ½ cup sugar ½ cup packed brown sugar	● In a large mixer bowl beat butter or margarine with electric mixer on medium speed about 30 seconds or till butter is softened. Add sugar and brown sugar; beat till fluffy.
1 egg 1 teaspoon vanilla	● Add egg and vanilla. Beat well.
1¼ cups all-purpose flour ½ teaspoon baking soda ½ teaspoon baking powder	● In a medium mixing bowl stir together flour, baking soda, and baking powder. With mixer on low speed gradually add the flour mixture to the butter mixture, beating till well mixed.
1 3½-ounce can (1⅓ cups) flaked coconut 1 cup wheat flakes *or* four-grain cereal flakes 1 cup raisins *or* semisweet chocolate pieces	● Stir in coconut, cereal, and raisins or chocolate pieces. Drop by rounded teaspoons about 2 inches apart onto ungreased cookie sheets. Bake in a 375° oven for 8 to 10 minutes or till golden. Cool about 1 minute before removing to a wire rack; cool. Makes about 72 cookies.

This recipe makes about six dozen cookies. That's a lot of cookies unless there are lots of cookie lovers around. You can freeze some of the cookies for longer storage. Just pack them in freezer containers with waxed paper between the layers. They'll wait patiently till you need them for a no-fuss treat.

Peanut-Oatmeal Double-Dealers

¼ **cup shortening**
¼ **cup peanut butter**
¼ **cup sugar**
¼ **cup packed brown sugar**

● In a medium mixing bowl use a wooden spoon to mix together the shortening and peanut butter. Add sugar and brown sugar. Stir till well mixed.

These oatmeal cookies are doubly good because you make them with both peanut butter and chopped peanuts.

1 **egg**
2 **tablespoons milk**
½ **teaspoon vanilla**

● Add the egg, milk, and vanilla. Stir till well mixed.

½ **cup all-purpose flour**
¼ **teaspoon baking soda**

● In a bowl stir together the flour and baking soda. Stir into the peanut butter mixture till well mixed.

⅓ **cup quick-cooking rolled oats**
⅓ **cup chopped peanuts**

● Stir in the oats and peanuts. Drop by rounded teaspoons about 2 inches apart onto greased cookie sheets.

Bake in a 375° oven for 8 to 10 minutes or till golden. Remove from cookie sheets. Cool on a wire rack. Makes about 32.

Peanut-Oatmeal Double-Dealers

Hay and Gravel Bars
(see recipe, page 52)

Freckled Cocoa Cookies
(see recipe, page 56)

Flannel Jammies
(see recipe, page 53)

Pucker Bars
(see recipe, page 55)

Wacky Cracker Cake

About 14 graham cracker squares	● Finely crush the graham cracker squares to make 1 cup crumbs. Empty crumbs into a small mixing bowl.
3 tablespoons all-purpose flour 1 teaspoon baking powder	● Stir flour and baking powder into graham cracker crumbs. Set aside.
¼ cup butter *or* margarine ⅓ cup sugar 1 egg ½ teaspoon vanilla	● In a small mixer bowl beat butter or margarine with an electric mixer on medium speed about 30 seconds or till softened. Add sugar and beat till fluffy. Add egg and vanilla; beat well.
½ cup milk ⅓ cup mixed dried fruit bits Powdered sugar	● Add the graham cracker mixture and milk alternately to butter mixture, beating till smooth. Stir in the dried fruit. Spoon into a greased and floured 7½x3½x2-inch loaf pan. Bake in a 350° oven 30 to 35 minutes or till a wooden toothpick inserted in center comes out clean. Cool in pan on a wire rack 10 minutes. Remove; cool. Sprinkle with powdered sugar. Serves 8.

Crushing graham crackers is one way a kid can help with this recipe. First, put the crackers in a large plastic bag and put that bag inside another large plastic bag. Squeeze out the excess air and tie the end of the doubled bag. Now hand your helper a rolling pin to roll over the crackers till they're crushed to smithereens.

Roundabout Banana Cake

1½ cups all-purpose flour ¾ cup sugar ¾ teaspoon baking powder ½ teaspoon salt ¼ teaspoon baking soda	● In a mixing bowl stir together flour, sugar, baking powder, salt, and baking soda. Make a well in the center.
2 beaten eggs 2 medium bananas, mashed (⅔ cup) ⅓ cup cooking oil ¼ cup milk ½ teaspoon vanilla	● In another bowl combine beaten eggs, mashed bananas, cooking oil, milk, and vanilla. Add all at once to the flour mixture, stirring till well mixed.
½ cup miniature semisweet chocolate pieces *or* semisweet chocolate pieces	● Stir in chocolate pieces. Spoon the batter into a greased and floured 5½- or 6-cup ring mold. Bake in a 350° oven about 35 minutes or till a wooden toothpick inserted between center and edge comes out clean. Cool in ring mold on a wire rack 10 minutes. Remove; cool completely. Makes 8 to 10 servings.

This cake was a winner with our discriminating panel of 10- and 11-year-olds. Elizabeth said it tasted like banana bread with chocolate chips. Joy liked the ring shape of the cake and thought that it should be called *Roundabout Banana Cake*. We thought so, too.

Wacky Cracker Cake

Roundabout Banana Cake

Carrot Cupcakes
(see recipe, page 62)

Adam's Apple Cake
(see recipe, page 62)

Topsy-Turvy Crunch Cake
(see recipe, page 64)

Adam's Apple Cake

Pictured on page 61.

1¼ cups all-purpose flour ½ teaspoon baking soda ½ teaspoon ground cinnamon ¼ teaspoon salt ¼ cup butter *or* margarine	● In a medium mixing bowl combine flour, baking soda, cinnamon, and salt. Cut in butter or margarine till the mixture resembles coarse crumbs.
1 beaten egg ½ cup applesauce ⅓ cup light molasses	● In a small mixing bowl stir together egg, applesauce, and molasses; stir into flour mixture just till moistened.
¼ cup raisins	● Stir in raisins. Turn into a greased and floured 8x8x2-inch baking pan. Bake in a 350° oven for 25 to 30 minutes or till a wooden toothpick inserted in the center comes out clean. Cool in the pan 15 minutes. Remove from pan, if desired.
¾ cup sifted powdered sugar 4 teaspoons lemon juice	● Combine powdered sugar and lemon juice; spread over warm cake. Serve warm or cool. Makes 9 servings.

Applesauce, a favorite with most kids, gives this snack cake its moistness and makes it a good keeper. With hungry snackers around, however, you may never find out how well it stores.

Carrot Cupcakes

Pictured on page 61.

1 4½-ounce jar strained carrots (baby food) ¼ cup packed brown sugar 1 egg 2 tablespoons cooking oil ⅛ teaspoon finely shredded orange peel	● In a small mixing bowl reserve *1 tablespoon* of the strained carrots for frosting; cover and set aside. In a medium mixing bowl combine remaining carrots, brown sugar, egg, oil, and ⅛ teaspoon orange peel; beat with a wire whisk or fork till smooth.
1 cup packaged biscuit mix	● Add biscuit mix; beat just till mixed. Spoon into greased or paper-bake-cup-lined muffin cups, filling two-thirds full. Bake in a 375° oven for 15 to 20 minutes or till a wooden toothpick inserted in center comes out clean. Remove cupcakes. Cool on a wire rack.
1 tablespoon butter *or* margarine, softened ⅛ teaspoon finely shredded orange peel ½ to ¾ cup sifted powdered sugar	● For frosting, add softened butter or margarine and ⅛ teaspoon orange peel to the reserved carrots. Gradually stir in enough powdered sugar to make of spreading consistency. Frost cupcakes. Makes 6.

No need to shred carrots for these little carrot cakes! Take the easy route and use a jar of baby food instead.

Pumpkin Bumpkins

1 package 1-layer-size spice cake mix 1 cup canned pumpkin 1 egg 2 tablespoons milk	● In a small mixer bowl combine spice cake mix, pumpkin, egg, and milk. Beat with an electric mixer on medium speed till well mixed.	**The flavor of these cupcakes reminded Jeremy, one of our taste-testers, of the pumpkin cake his grandma makes. But he had never seen cupcakes made into sandwiches before.**
	● Spoon batter into greased muffin cups, filling two-thirds full. Bake in a 350° oven about 20 minutes or till a wooden toothpick inserted in center comes out clean. Remove cupcakes from pans. Cool on a wire rack.	
Plain soft-style cream cheese *or* soft-style cream cheese with pineapple ½ cup raisins	● With a serrated knife, cut cooled cupcakes in half horizontally. Spread the bottom half of each cupcake with cream cheese. Sprinkle with raisins. Top with the other half. Makes 10 cupcakes.	

Freezing Cakes and Cupcakes

When everyone has had his fill and there's still some cake left over, freeze it as a ready-made treat for later. Cakes can be frozen both plain and already frosted, but frosted cakes may become soggy when you thaw them.

To freeze unfrosted cakes or cupcakes, wrap them in moisture- and vaporproof wrap; seal, label, and freeze up to 6 months. Thaw the cake in the wrap at room temperature. Allow about 40 minutes for cupcakes to thaw and up to 1 hour for one-layer cakes.

For cakes or cupcakes that are frosted, freeze them first and then wrap. This will keep the wrap from sticking to the frosting. Thaw frosted or filled cakes, covered, in the refrigerator several hours or overnight.

Topsy-Turvy Crunch Cake

Pictured on page 61.

3 tablespoons butter *or* margarine 2 tablespoons brown sugar 1 tablespoon honey	● In a saucepan heat the butter or margarine, brown sugar, and honey over medium-low heat till butter is melted. Remove from heat.
¼ cup flaked coconut ¼ cup unsalted sunflower nuts *or* chopped peanuts 1½ teaspoons water ½ teaspoon vanilla	● Stir in coconut, sunflower nuts or chopped peanuts, water, and vanilla. Spread the coconut mixture evenly in a greased 9x1½-inch round baking pan.
1 package 1-layer-size yellow cake mix	● Prepare cake mix batter according to package directions; pour over the coconut mixture in the pan. Bake in a 350° oven for 25 to 30 minutes or till a wooden toothpick inserted in the center comes out clean. Cool on a wire rack for 10 minutes. Invert cake onto rack. Spread any topping left in the pan onto cake. Cool. Makes 6 to 8 servings.

Ten minutes after the cake comes out of the oven, have the kids watch you flip it out of the pan. The sweet and nutty topping that was on the bottom of the cake turns out on top.

Mole Hole Cupcakes

Pictured on page 4.

1 beaten egg ½ cup peach yogurt 1 package 1-layer-size yellow cake mix	● In a small mixing bowl combine egg and yogurt; stir in cake mix just till moistened. Spoon batter into lightly greased or paper-bake-cup-lined muffin cups, filling each half full.
2 tablespoons apricot *or* peach preserves	● Spoon ½ *teaspoon* of the preserves into the center of *each* cupcake, as shown at right.
2 tablespoons toasted wheat germ	● Sprinkle ½ *teaspoon* wheat germ over *each* cupcake. Bake in a 350° oven about 25 minutes or till a wooden toothpick inserted near center (in cake, not in the preserves) comes out clean. Remove from pans. Cool on a wire rack. Makes 12.

Spoon preserves into the center of the batter in each muffin cup. When the cupcakes are baked, you'll see a hole in the top, just like 10-year-old Hawkeye did when he gave these cupcakes their clever name.

Snowflake Cake

1½ cups all-purpose flour
1 cup sugar
¼ cup unsweetened cocoa
powder
1 teaspoon baking soda
½ teaspoon salt
¼ teaspoon ground
cinnamon

● In a medium mixing bowl stir together flour, sugar, unsweetened cocoa powder, baking soda, salt, and cinnamon. Make a well in the center of the flour mixture.

This chocolate cake is so moist it doesn't need frosting. Instead, top it with a snowflake—one that you make with powdered sugar and the help of a paper doily.

⅓ cup cooking oil
1 tablespoon vinegar
1 teaspoon vanilla
1 cup cold water

● Pour oil, vinegar, and vanilla into the well in the flour mixture. Pour the cold water over all. Stir with a spoon till ingredients are moistened.
Pour the batter into a greased 8x8x2-inch baking pan. Bake in a 350° oven for 25 to 30 minutes or till a wooden toothpick inserted in center comes out clean. Cool in the pan on a wire rack.

8-inch-diameter paper
doily
Powdered sugar

● Place the paper doily on top of the cooled cake. Sift powdered sugar over the cake. Carefully lift off the doily, as shown below. Makes 16 servings.

To make the snowflake on the top of the cake, put an 8-inch paper doily on the cake top. Sift powdered sugar over the top. Carefully lift off the doily, making sure the powdered sugar on the doily doesn't fall through the holes and mess up the design.

Peanutty Fudge

½ cup peanut butter
¼ cup milk
1 teaspoon vanilla
2¼ cups sifted powdered sugar
½ cup unsweetened cocoa powder
½ cup finely chopped peanuts

● In a large mixer bowl beat together peanut butter, milk, and vanilla. Gradually beat in *1¼ cups* of the powdered sugar and the cocoa powder. Stir in peanuts. Stir in remaining powdered sugar.

● Turn out onto a work surface and knead till well blended. Press into a foil-lined 8x8x2-inch baking pan; cut into 1-inch squares. Or, shape into ¾-inch balls. Makes about 1⅓ pounds.

Grown-ups like this fudge because there's no cooking to do. Kids like it because it's creamy, peanutty, and melts in their mouths.

One recipe will make sixty-four 1-inch squares or forty-five ¾-inch balls.

Calico Caramel Corn

8 cups fruit-flavored corn puff cereal

● Place corn puff cereal in a 15x10x1-inch baking pan. Set aside.

½ cup packed brown sugar
6 tablespoons butter *or* margarine
3 tablespoons light corn syrup
¼ teaspoon salt

● In a 1½-quart saucepan combine brown sugar, butter or margarine, corn syrup, and salt. Cook and stir over medium heat till butter is melted and mixture comes to boiling. Cook, without stirring, for 5 minutes more. Remove from heat.

½ teaspoon vanilla
¼ teaspoon baking soda

● Stir vanilla and baking soda into mixture in saucepan. Pour over cereal; stir to coat evenly.
    Bake in a 300° oven for 15 minutes. Stir. Bake 5 to 10 minutes more. Transfer cereal to a large bowl. Cool. Store in a tightly covered container. Makes 8 cups.

Instead of popcorn, this caramel corn is made with multicolored puffed corn cereal. Keep it in a tightly covered container so it keeps its crunch.

Honeybees

EQUIPMENT

mixing bowl	waxed paper
measuring cups	baking sheet
measuring spoons	toothpick
wooden spoon	

½ cup peanut butter
1 tablespoon honey

● In a mixing bowl use a wooden spoon to mix the peanut butter and honey.

⅓ cup nonfat dry milk powder
2 tablespoons sesame seed
2 tablespoons toasted wheat germ

● Stir in the dry milk powder, sesame seed, and wheat germ till well mixed.

Unsweetened cocoa powder
Sliced almonds

● Lay waxed paper on a baking sheet. Using a teaspoon at a time, shape the peanut butter mixture into ovals to look like bees. Put on the baking sheet. Dip a toothpick in cocoa powder, then press gently across top of bees to make stripes.

Stick in almonds for wings. Chill in the refrigerator 30 minutes. Makes 28.

This snack attracts kids like bees to a blossom. It could be that kids like shaping the bees or making the cocoa powder stripes. It could be they like the almond wings. But we think it's the honey-peanut flavor that keeps kids buzzing around for more.

Oatmeal Chews

¾ **cup packed brown sugar** ½ **cup butter *or* margarine**	● In a medium saucepan combine brown sugar and butter or margarine. Cook and stir till butter is melted.
2 cups quick-cooking rolled oats **1 teaspoon baking powder**	● Stir in quick-cooking rolled oats and baking powder. Mix well. Spread mixture in a well-greased 8x8x2-inch baking pan. Bake in a 350° oven about 18 minutes or till golden. (Center will still be soft.) Cool on a wire rack. Cut into bars. Makes 24.

These simple bars are sweet like candy but chewy like cookies. Elizabeth, one of our young tasters, said that they reminded her of granola bars.

Roly-Polies

½ **of a 3-ounce package**
    cream cheese, softened
¼ **teaspoon lemon *or***
    peppermint extract
	● In a small mixer bowl beat softened cream cheese and lemon or peppermint extract with electric mixer on medium speed till well mixed.

1½ cups sifted powdered sugar	● Gradually beat in powdered sugar till smooth, kneading in the last of the powdered sugar with your hands.
1 *or* 2 drops food coloring	● Knead in the food coloring till evenly colored. Chill if necessary. Shape into ¾-inch balls.
¼ **cup sugar**	● Place sugar in a shallow dish. Roll balls in sugar. Chill till ready to serve. Makes about 24.

After you decide whether to make your *Roly-Polies* lemon- or mint-flavored, choose the color you want them to be. If you like, divide the uncolored mixture into several bowls and tint each portion a different color.

Roly-Polies can be frozen up to one month. Thaw before serving.

Peanut Butter Fingers

EQUIPMENT

medium mixing bowl	plastic sandwich bag
measuring cups	small spoon
measuring spoons	waxed paper
large spoon	pie plate

⅓ cup peanut butter
3 tablespoons honey

● In a medium mixing bowl use a large spoon to stir together the peanut butter and honey till smooth.

½ cup corn flakes
½ cup quick-cooking rolled oats
¼ cup nonfat dry milk powder
¼ cup mixed dried fruit bits

● Put corn flakes in a plastic sandwich bag. Close the open end. With your fist, crush the corn flakes into small pieces.
　Add corn flakes, oats, dry milk powder, and fruit to the peanut butter mixture in the bowl. With your hands, mix well. If mixture is too dry to hold together, mix in a few drops of water.

Sesame seed *or* toasted wheat germ

● Using a well-rounded teaspoon for each, shape into logs 2 inches long and ½ inch wide, or about the size of your finger. Put on a piece of waxed paper.
　Spread the sesame seed or wheat germ in a pie plate. Roll peanut butter fingers in the sesame seed or wheat germ. Store in an airtight container in the refrigerator. Makes about 20.

When five-year-old Aleisha came to our kitchens to test several recipes, she liked this one best of all. She liked it *so* well that her mother called later that day to get the recipe. Aleisha didn't want to wait till the book was finished to make this finger-lickin' snack.

Flip-Flop Bars

½ cup peanut butter
¼ cup light corn syrup
2 tablespoons sugar
1½ cups crisp rice cereal

● Line an 8x8x2-inch baking pan with foil. Butter foil. In a medium saucepan combine peanut butter, ¼ cup corn syrup, and 2 tablespoons sugar. Cook over low heat till peanut butter is melted. Stir in 1½ cups cereal till well coated.
　Transfer peanut butter-cereal mixture to the foil-lined pan. Press mixture evenly into the pan.

1 6-ounce package (1 cup) semisweet chocolate pieces
¼ cup light corn syrup
2 tablespoons sugar
2 tablespoons butter *or* margarine
1½ cups crisp rice cereal

● In the same saucepan combine chocolate pieces, ¼ cup corn syrup, 2 tablespoons sugar, and butter or margarine. Cook and stir over low heat till chocolate and butter are melted. Stir in 1½ cups cereal till well coated.
　Spread chocolate-cereal mixture evenly atop peanut butter-cereal mixture. Cool. Cut into squares. Makes 16.

Pictured on page 5.

Chocolate on one side and peanut butter on the other, this crispy cereal snack was a hit with the kids. One taster named Aaron gave us his opinion about the bars in one word: "Wow!"

Strawberry Cheesecake Sandwiches

EQUIPMENT
table knife

This is the easiest snack in the whole book!

**Soft-style cream cheese (plain, with strawberry, *or* with pineapple)
Vanilla wafers**

● With a table knife spread some of the cream cheese on the flat side of a vanilla wafer. Top with another vanilla wafer, flat side down. Eat right away.

Shaky Shapes

1½ **cups water**
3 **envelopes unflavored gelatin**

● Pour the water into a medium saucepan. Sprinkle the gelatin over the water. Let stand 1 minute.
   Bring mixture to boiling, stirring constantly till gelatin dissolves. Remove from heat.

Kids will have a good time cutting this wiggly treat into crazy shapes. But here's the best part of all: It's a great way to sooth a child's sweet tooth without dipping into the sugar bowl.

1 **6-ounce can frozen apple, cranberry, orange, tangerine, *or* grape juice concentrate**

● Stir in frozen juice concentrate. Stir till juice concentrate is melted.
   Pour mixture into a foil-lined 8x8x2-inch baking pan. Cover and chill till firm.

● Invert the gelatin mixture onto a cutting board. Remove the foil. Use cookie cutters or a table knife to cut the gelatin into shapes. Makes about 36 (1½-inch) pieces.

This Little Pig

1 whole watermelon	● Cut a large opening in the top of the watermelon, cutting out a spiral tail, if desired. Remove cut-out section. Cut a 2-inch-diameter circle from the cut-out section; reserve for snout. From remainder of cutout, cut 2 triangles; reserve for ears.
	● With a melon ball cutter, scoop out watermelon balls and place in a large bowl, removing seeds as you go. Scrape out and discard remaining melon on inside walls. Invert melon shell; drain.
1 medium cantaloupe **2 cups seedless grapes** **1 15¼-ounce can pineapple chunks (juice pack), drained**	● Remove seeds from the cantaloupe. Scoop out cantaloupe balls; add to the watermelon in the large bowl. Add the grapes and pineapple chunks. Gently stir to mix. Cover and chill.
2 limes	● Meanwhile, decorate the outside of the watermelon. Cut the limes in half crosswise. If desired, remove a strip of peel from limes as shown. Attach lime halves with toothpicks to lower side of watermelon for feet.
1 maraschino cherry, halved	● With toothpicks attach reserved circle for snout. Attach reserved watermelon triangles, point side up, for ears. Attach cherry halves for eyes.
	● Before serving, drain any liquid from fruit. Transfer the fruit to the watermelon shell. To serve, spoon fruit into cups or bowls. Trim with decorative toothpicks, if desired. Makes 24 to 32 servings.

This Little Pig wants to have a party and he wants lots of kids to come. His watermelon body is filled with juicy pieces of fruit that are just the right size for little mouths. He likes parties that are outside or somewhere not too fancy so no one has to worry about dripping or dropping the fruit.

To help you cut out the curly tail, draw the tail on the watermelon rind before you cut. A different way to make a tail is to peel a whole lime, keeping the peel in one piece. Attach it to the watermelon with a toothpick.

Indian Corn

10 cups popped popcorn (½ cup unpopped) ½ cup dried apricots	● Put popcorn in a large roasting pan; keep warm in a 300° oven. Finely chop dried apricots; set aside.	*Indian Corn* is always in season, but it's extra nice for fall weather fun such as a Thanksgiving or Halloween party. These oblong popcorn balls on sticks will keep 12 little Indians munching happily.
1 cup packed brown sugar ¾ cup water ¼ cup light corn syrup ¾ teaspoon vinegar	● In a small saucepan combine brown sugar, water, corn syrup, and vinegar. Cook and stir over medium-high heat till the mixture boils over the entire surface. Continue cooking to 250° (hard-ball stage), stirring frequently. (This will take 15 to 20 minutes after the mixture comes to boiling.)	
½ cup raisins 12 wooden sticks	● Pour sugar mixture over popcorn. Immediately stir in apricots and raisins till all ingredients are coated. Using buttered hands, shape mixture into 4-inch-long sticks resembling ears of corn. (If mixture is too firm to shape, return it to the warm oven for 1 to 2 minutes to soften.) Insert a wooden stick into the end of each. Serve the same day. Makes 12.	

Tangled Bread

Pictured on page 5.

1 16-ounce loaf frozen whole wheat bread dough, thawed	● On a floured surface roll the dough into a 12x6-inch rectangle, allowing dough to rest during rolling, if necessary.	These chewy pretzels make a neat, non-sweet party treat. The kids at our tasting party suggested spreading the pretzels with cream cheese, peanut butter, or cheese spread.
	● Cut into twelve 6x1-inch strips. Roll into ropes about 14 inches long. Shape each pretzel by crossing one end over the other to form a circle, overlapping about 3½ inches from each end (A). Take one end in each hand and twist once where dough overlaps (B). Carefully lift ends across to opposite edge of circle. Tuck ends under edge (C). Moisten and press ends to seal. Place pretzels 1 inch apart on a well-greased baking sheet. Let stand, uncovered, for 20 minutes.	To reheat the pretzels for serving warm, heat on a baking sheet in a 350° oven about 2 minutes or till warm.
1 egg 1 tablespoon water Sesame seed, poppy seed, *or* toasted wheat germ	● Beat together egg and water. With a pastry brush, brush tops of pretzels with egg mixture. Sprinkle with sesame seed, poppy seed, or wheat germ. Bake in a 350° oven for 18 to 20 minutes or till golden brown. Remove; cool on a wire rack. Makes 12.	

A   B   C

Zucchini Zoo

● Set out zucchini Bodies and the vegetable Heads. Let children attach heads to bodies with toothpicks to make animals.
● Set out a container of *soft-style cream cheese*. Let children attach Body Stick-Ons with the cream cheese and more toothpicks, if necessary, to give the animals legs, feet, noses, eyes, tails, etc.
● To eat, remove toothpicks and eat vegetable animals.

Bodies

Small zucchini, cut into
  2-inch pieces

+ Heads

Small zucchini, cut into
  1-inch pieces
Whole radishes
Whole small pickles,
  halved crosswise

+ Body Stick-Ons

Carrots, some cut into
  ½-inch slices, some cut
  into 2-inch pieces, and
  some chopped
Whole small pickles
Pickle slices
Pimiento-stuffed olives,
  halved
Sliced celery
Chopped nuts
Sliced almonds
Slivered almonds
Raisins
Chow mein noodles
Round toasted oat cereal
  or other ready-to-eat
  cereal

Fancy Hats

Pictured on page 5.

1 quart ice cream *or* sherbet 12 crisp sugar cookies, oatmeal cookies, *or* other cookies (at least 3 inches in diameter)	● Let ice cream or sherbet stand at room temperature just till slightly softened. Place cookies on a cookie sheet. Using a ⅓-cup ice cream scoop, place one scoop ice cream atop each cookie. Freeze 20 minutes or till ice cream is firm.
Pressurized dessert topping Small multicolored flower-shape decorative candies 1 tube brown decorator icing and plastic writing tip Slivered almonds	● To decorate, remove a few at a time. For ladies' hats, pipe a ring of dessert topping around base of ice cream; decorate one side with candies. For men's hats, pipe a ring of brown decorator icing around base of ice cream; decorate one side with slivered almonds to resemble feathers. Return decorated hats to freezer. Repeat with remaining. Makes 12 servings.

Edible hats are a great dessert for a kids' dress-up party. Before the party, send out formal invitations telling your guests to wear fancy grown-up clothes their parents will let them play in. When they arrive, have an adult dressed as a butler or a maid welcome them at the door. When it's time for dessert, have the butler or maid serve the ladies a flowery hat and the gentlemen a feathered hat.

Bow Ties

12 slices soft-texture bread	● With a serrated knife, trim crusts from bread slices.
American cheese spread	● Spread a thin layer of cheese spread on the bread slices.
6 slices bacon	● Cut each bacon slice in half crosswise. Roll up a bread slice jelly-roll style with cheese on the inside, as shown below. Wrap a bacon piece around center. Repeat with remaining bread and bacon. Place on a baking sheet with overlapped ends of bacon on bottom. Bake in a 400° oven about 12 minutes or till bread is toasted and bacon is crisp. Remove. Serve warm. Makes 12.

Bow Ties **are definitely proper at a make-believe dress-up party. Your "formally attired" guests will rave about these wrapped-up grilled cheese sandwiches.**

After you've spread the bread with cheese, roll it up with the cheese on the inside. Wrap a bacon piece around the middle. As the bacon cooks, it will squeeze the bread slightly to look like a bow tie.

Stuffed Puffs

1 16-ounce loaf frozen bread dough, thawed	● On a floured surface divide the dough into 16 equal pieces. Pat each piece into a 3-inch circle.
1 8-ounce fully cooked ham slice, cut 1 inch thick; one 7-ounce can luncheon meat; *or* 3 or 4 frankfurters ¾ cup shredded cheddar cheese (3 ounces)	● Cut ham slice or luncheon meat into sixteen 1-inch cubes or cut frankfurters into sixteen 1-inch slices. Place a piece of meat on a dough circle. Sprinkle with a rounded teaspoon of the cheese. Pull dough up and around the meat and cheese to form a ball; pinch with your fingers to seal. Repeat with remaining dough, meat, and cheese.
	● Place balls, seam side down, on a greased baking sheet. Cover; let rise in a warm place about 30 minutes or till nearly double. (Or, cover loosely with plastic wrap. Refrigerate 3 to 24 hours. Before baking, remove from refrigerator. Uncover and let stand 10 minutes.) Bake in a 350° oven for 25 to 30 minutes or till puffs are golden. Serve warm. Makes 16.

Turn treat time into a treasure hunt with these balloonlike party sandwiches. In one of the puffs, enclose a whole shelled almond, a pecan half, or a pickle slice instead of the meat. Whoever gets the puff with the nut or pickle in it gets a prize for finding the treasure.

Upside-Down Sundaes

2 cups milk ½ cup peanut butter 1 package 4-serving-size *instant* chocolate pudding mix	● In a small mixer bowl combine milk and peanut butter. Beat with an electric mixer on low speed till almost blended. Add chocolate pudding mix; beat according to package directions, scraping sides of bowl frequently. Pour ¼ *cup* of the pudding mixture into 10 individual dessert dishes.
10 scoops vanilla ice cream ½ cup chopped peanuts	● Top each with a scoop of ice cream. Sprinkle with peanuts. Serves 10.

Make your next party an upside-down party! Address and write the invitations upside down. At the party, set plates and cups bottoms up and turn pictures on the wall upside down. For treats, serve these sundaes that have chocolate pudding on the bottom and ice cream on top.

Index